Grief
Country

Also by Stephanie Larkin

Displaced: A Memoir

Pain Power Purpose: A Story of
Trauma-Informed Healing

Widowed in Seattle: Local Resources
and Information

Life Love Loss: A Poetry Chapbook

Resettled

Introduction to Chizigula

Chizigula-English Book 1

Grief
Country

STEPHANIE LARKIN

AHADI PUBLICATIONS
Olympia, Washington

Published by Ahadi Publications
Olympia, Washington

Cover Photo: Pixabay

Library of Congress Control Number: 2018940843

ISBN: 978-0-9976983-3-6

Printed in the United States of America

First printing, 2018

For Ron and Virginia

"Great grief is a divine and terrible radiance

which transfigures the wretched."

Victor Hugo

CONTENTS

Introduction

PART I – UNDERSTANDING

Grief Country /5
A Ghost Walking Backwards /8
Anticipatory Grief / 9
Crossing Over / 19
Normal Grief / 21
One Hundred Years of Grief / 31
Haiku for Ron / 40
When Grief is Not "Normal" / 41
Haunted / 49
Anger / 50
Ghost Town / 56

PART II – COPING

Who Am I Now? / 58
The 6.5 Percent / 64
Resilience and Rebuilding / 68
Finding My Own Song / 75
Duty of Care / 78
Great Expectations /81
Letting Go / 90
Credentials / 98
The Wild West / 100
Aftershocks / 107
A Show of Hands / 109
Step-Widowhood / 114
Dancing / 124

CONTENTS

PART III – REFLECTING

Experts (Part 1) / 129
The Second Worst / 137
A Moment of Silence / 146
Metamorphosis / 150
Social Media / 151
Research Has Shown... / 155
Psst! Tell Your Friend / 163
Experts (Part 2) / 170
The Chain / 174
Building Bridges / 175
The Road / 180
Far Pavilions / 182

Afterword / 191
Notes / 193

INTRODUCTION

Every road that leads to widowhood follows its own heartbreaking course. My journey took me on a frightening and fast-moving ride across territory I never imagined I would ever set eyes upon: the land of aggressive, malignant brain cancer.

On Christmas Day 2010 my husband Ron appeared to be in fairly good health; two weeks later he was diagnosed with glioblastoma multiforme, the most lethal type of brain cancer. Without treatment, the doctor said he might live three months. With treatment, perhaps a year—no guarantees.

As my husband valiantly battled glioblastoma, I began experiencing loss. One small loss after another, culminating in the Loss with a capital "L" that I had dreaded for more than a year. I was so overwhelmed by what I was feeling that after my husband died, I began to study the subject of grief. If I could just *understand* more, I thought, maybe I could lessen this searing pain.

Studying grief was not the answer to my pain but it was a distraction, allowing me to step away at times from the sharply visceral experience and seclude myself in an ivory tower of detached intellectual contemplation.

During my off-and-on study of grief, I purchased many books, downloaded dozens of articles from the internet, and spent hours among the stacks of reference materials and psychology journals in the library of a large state university. I steered clear of memoirs, instead focusing only on books that were analytical and research-based, usually written by psychologists and psychiatrists. This decision did not reflect any negativity about memoirs, only a desire to keep my focus on learning what the experts had to say about grief. I also recognized that as a fresh widow, I wasn't necessarily in the position of being able to enter into another widow's pain to any great extent.

As time permitted, I began writing about my experience. A poem here, an essay there… I stabbed at my grief with my pen. Like so many widows, I was filled with the desire to give voice to my overwhelming emotions.

This book is a glimpse into my personal journey of loss. It includes a number of poems and essays that were written during my first five years of widowhood; my reflections about some of the theories of grief that have been put forth by experts over the years; and my thoughts on a myriad of issues surrounding bereavement.

In some cases I note the year I wrote a particular poem or essay to provide context. The rest of the book was written during my fourth and fifth years of widowhood.

At times in this book I refer to conversations with other widows. The excerpts of the conversations I've had with my friends and acquaintances are real, but out of respect for their privacy, their names have been omitted or changed. I have not included any stories that were shared in my presence in grief support groups where there was an expectation of privacy except in a most general fashion, where, for example, I might refer to a particular issue as being a common concern among widows.

I have written about my own experience of losing a husband to a terminal illness. I couldn't begin to describe or understand what it's like to lose a husband under other circumstances (such as an accident, sudden death, suicide, or homicide), so I don't address those losses. Although some of the information or observations presented in this book might apply to those who are grieving a death other than that of a husband, my focus was on widowhood.

Many highly credentialed and dedicated individuals have devoted their lives to the study of grief. There is no way to do justice to the work that has been poured into this subject, so the brief references I make to a limited number of experts and theories are merely my attempts to "hit the highlights" in an effort to provide the reader with a general overview of this field of study.

It was nearly impossible to write this book without occasionally stumbling off the road of personal experience and into the ditch of overgeneralizing, so I ask the reader to take that into consideration if in certain passages I appear to be painting a picture of widows with too broad a brush.

Every widow has a unique story, a unique set of challenges, and a unique path forward. I hope that sharing my own story might help to increase understanding of the shattering experience of widowhood and offer hope to some of those who have suddenly found themselves living in Grief Country.

PART I

UNDERSTANDING

DEFINITIONS

BEREAVEMENT: The state or fact of being bereaved or deprived of something or someone.

GRIEF: Deep and poignant distress caused by bereavement.

MOURNING: 1) The act of sorrowing; 2) an outward sign...of grief for a person's death; 3) a period of time during which signs of grief are shown.

Merriam-Webster Dictionary

GRIEF COUNTRY
(An essay written at the end of Year Two)

I picture grief as a country.

Within the borders of Grief Country are dozens of states, and I have visited most of them. I've traveled to the State of Numbness (a short visit), the State of Sadness (I still return there often), and the State of Anger (sometimes stopping to visit its state capital, Screaming-at-God-in-the-Car).

I passed quickly through the State of Denial, barely pausing to look around. I had already visited that particular state fairly frequently during the early days of my husband's terminal brain cancer diagnosis, so it had little to offer me.

It can be exhausting for a widow, jetting around Grief Country. Even though some have wanted to accompany me, that's not the way it works in Grief Country. Ultimately, my widowed friends and I must take solo journeys. No one sits in the jump seat.

Our loved ones may not even realize that we have logged thousands upon thousands of miles in the battered little aircraft they cannot see. They may not understand why we are always so jet-lagged, unsure at times which time zone we're in, dragging around suitcases weighed down with memories, history, and fears of an unknown future.

At America's Four Corners Monument, tourists are able to stand in Arizona, New Mexico, Colorado, and Utah simultaneously. So it is with Grief Country, where at times it seems as if I'm straddling several states at once... one foot on the border between the State of Fatigue and the State of Anxiety, the other foot on the border between the State of Social Withdrawal and the State of Self-Absorption.

Even though my widowed friends can't travel with me, we do keep track of each other's journeys, and sometimes we cross paths, finding ourselves in the same state at the same time. We console each other and compare notes about our travels. None of us wanted to become members of this reluctant frequent-flyer club, but there is a small comfort in numbers.

After two years, I think I've seen most of what Grief Country has to offer, but it seems as if I no sooner proclaim to friends that I think I'm done traveling than I'm spirited away without warning, transported back to one of the now-familiar states— like the State of Vulnerability or the State of Depression.

Thankfully, I don't linger as long on most of my sojourns as I did early on, but I've learned that even though my stays may be brief, I will most likely be flying around Grief Country for a long time—quite possibly for the rest of my life.

So many planes in the air. I suppose we don't really notice how crowded the skies are until we've entered Grief Country.

A GHOST WALKING BACKWARDS

Behind these steel bars we mark the days
One brain MRI at a time
The prison break we'd hoped to pull off
now a dream surrendered

He is a shadow of himself
A ghost walking backwards—
away from my outstretched hand
but never beyond true love's grasp

I remember for both of us

The hand that once held mine
as we strolled the shoreline
Now a rigid fist, fingers curled to his chest
Pressed against the heart he claimed I stole

I clasp his narrow shoulders
Weary eyes meet mine
Desperation falls from my lips
"Do you know me?" "Do you still love me?"

Lopsided smile
Eyes that almost twinkle still
Cherished words, softly spoken
"Always—
forever and beyond"

Stay of execution
My heart beats one more day

Scents of spring, blue skies beckoning
I dare not hear them call my name
as I fling the key far, far away

ANTICIPATORY GRIEF

From the moment my husband's doctor said he would most likely not survive brain cancer, I could feel my body change. Uncontrollable shaking and runaway adrenalin coursing through my veins, but at the same time, a feeling of paralysis. Then, like a shadow that blocks out the sun, the diagnosis immediately shrouded me in darkness, becoming a heavy black cloak that I could not shed no matter how hard I tried.

I had no idea at the time that I had just crossed the border into Grief Country and taken up residence in the State of Anticipatory Grief.

What is anticipatory grief?

The term was first coined by psychiatrist Erich Lindemann in 1944. Intrigued by the "enormous increase in grief reactions due to war casualties," he used the term to describe reactions of someone whose loved one was under "threat of death"; a soldier, for example. The person concerned for her loved one would be "going through all the phases of grief."[1]

Since that time many grief experts have redefined the term "anticipatory grief." Its application has shifted from those whose loved ones are under "threat of death" (a death which may or may not occur) to those whose loved ones have diagnosed, life-limiting illnesses. Most experts appear to have dropped Lindemann's reference to "phases of grief." Precise definitions vary between experts and they can be found by the dozens in numerous books and online, on websites and in articles.

In essence, however, anticipatory grief refers to reactions (emotions, thoughts, behaviors, physical responses) that are experienced by someone close to a person who is expected to die. These reactions can also be due to the myriad of losses that often occur prior to death, such as plans for a shared future.

(Anticipatory grief can also refer to the reactions of the person who is dying, but in this chapter I am referring to the reactions of the wife.)

During the time my husband Ron was ill, I was completely unaware of the term "anticipatory grief." It had not been mentioned in any of the literature provided by the hospital. Those handouts focused on dealing with cancer and mentioned caregiver stress, not grief in advance of certain death. The focus of the doctors was, understandably, their patient—not his wife.

What difference would it have made if I had known I was "grieving" during my husband's battle with terminal cancer rather than just feeling awful every minute of every day?

It would have given me a framework for my experience. I would have learned about the "symptoms" of anticipatory grief and realized I was not an anomaly; that what I was feeling was normal. It might have prompted me to consider counseling to deal with my overwhelming emotions.

Instead, during my husband's illness I put on the brave face that was expected. I was told how strong I was and how I was doing such a wonderful job of taking care of him. I desperately tried to control my emotions, but I was not always successful. A friend's criticism on the few occasions my suppressed anger erupted reinforced my belief that I needed to hide what I was feeling.

No one ever said, "It must be unbearable to know that the most important person in your life is going to die." Or "I can see how he has changed and that must be so difficult for you."

Just the opposite. No one wanted to acknowledge the fact that the rapidly growing tumor in my husband's brain was changing him… or acknowledge that I was already experiencing loss due to this change.

So the grief I was feeling went unaddressed.

What happens during anticipatory grief and how is it different from grief experienced after an actual death?

Many of the reactions are the same: sadness, shock, a sense of unreality, etc. The chapter entitled "Normal Grief" expands upon these reactions, which are sometimes controversially referred to as "symptoms." With anticipatory grief, however, there are additional reactions. Reflecting on my own experience and that of some of the widows I know who also lost their husbands after a long illness, those reactions included constant worry about our husband's health and anxiety over how their lives would end. *Will it be painful? How will I make sure it won't be? How can I handle watching him actually die?*

Some of us were traumatized by unforeseen events that took place—perhaps angry, violent outbursts from a husband whose illness affected his brain, or the shock of witnessing seizures, or finding him injured on the floor, or dealing with our spouse's adverse reactions to certain treatments. While these events might not have been of a magnitude to cause "post-traumatic stress," they might have been deeply disturbing, nonetheless.

Some of us had to learn how to master nursing responsibilities, such as administration of medications or oxygen, wound management, or assisting with physical therapy and occupational therapy exercises to keep him functioning as long as possible. Heel boots and catheters and morphine might have become part of our daily lives.

There is an element of grief that accompanies these new responsibilities (perhaps fighting back tears while struggling to physically lift the person who was once strong enough to carry us over the threshold on our wedding day), not to mention anxiety. *What if I'm not doing this correctly? What if I hurt him?*

We might have felt powerless as we watched our husbands slip away physically, and those of us who also watched them slip away mentally had to deal with that loss, too.

These are just a few personal observations of reactions that are different from grief after an actual death, but they are in line with the findings of many grief experts.

Within the hospice facility where my husband passed away was a small room with two shelves full of books about grief and loss. After his death I returned to the facility and borrowed a book entitled, *Living With Grief When Illness is Prolonged*, a collection of articles written by various grief experts, including Therese Rando, Ph.D. This book was my first exposure to the concept of "anticipatory grief."

In the article contributed by Rando, she mentioned the challenge for anticipatory grievers of "balancing of opposing needs."[2] I thought about how what my husband needed during his illness was not necessarily what I needed. For example, he did not need the social interaction that I missed.

Rando also mentions "guilt."[3] Although this is also a normal reaction after a death occurs, it takes on a different cast during anticipatory grief.

Guilt was the invisible duct tape that covered my mouth. What right did *I* have to feel bad or complain when my husband was the one with the death sentence hanging over his head? Especially when most of those around me embodied and prized stoicism.

Guilt can exist for all kinds of reasons. During Ron's illness I felt guilty that I was now anxious about my own future—*What's going to happen to me?*—when my husband had no future. I felt guilty during the times I felt frustration building. But most of all, I felt guilty that I hadn't figured out my husband had brain cancer earlier, which was ridiculous because he had so few symptoms of illness.

For those who are caring for a spouse with cognitive issues—perhaps late-stage Parkinson's, dementia, or, in my husband's case, brain cancer—there can be grief over finding ourselves "in charge" of everything, losing our equal partnership role (or whatever role we had). The intimacy that was taken for granted before might disappear overnight. Some of us discover that family and friends who supported us in the beginning might find it too uncomfortable or upsetting to be around our husbands as they continue to deteriorate physically and mentally. At the same time, our caregiving responsibilities mount, which makes it difficult to leave the home. The result is even more isolation, leaving us feeling utterly alone even though our husbands are nearby. Depression can gain a foothold.

And all this is *before* our husbands actually pass away.

After I became a widow, I read about "secondary losses," such as loss of identity and loss of financial security. For those who experience anticipatory grief, however, those "secondary" losses usually begin long before death occurs.

Before my husband died, we had already lost our income as he could no longer work. We had no choice but to sell our home at a significant financial loss. I had already lost my social connections and the identity I had established in the town we were forced to leave in order to pursue the best treatment for his illness.

For me, these losses were not "secondary." They were "anticipatory grief losses" that would merely continue into formal widowhood.

In light of all this grief and ongoing loss, a reader of this book might be able to understand how a comment such as "At least you had a chance to say goodbye" might be perceived as lacking in understanding, at best. The common assumption is that a dying husband and his wife are spending their days peacefully recalling their lives together, holding hands and gaining some sort of "closure" in advance of the inevitable death. While that may happen at some point, it doesn't necessarily reflect the reality of the overall experience of anticipatory grief for many women.

I will always be grateful for the time my husband and I had together during his illness. We certainly made the most of it, as his physical and mental health allowed. Caring for him was a privilege and honor, and I treasure not only the memories we created during our courtship and marriage, but the memories we created during the final months of his life. However, this is a book about grief, and my intention in this chapter is to be candid about my experience of anticipatory grief. Holding a hand and saying goodbye does not occur in a vacuum. Every touch, every word, is soaked in grief to some degree. I woke up every day to the strange bedfellows of gratitude and horror.

Even as I digested all the new information I was reading about anticipatory grief, I discovered that the term is not universally accepted by all grief experts.

Some maintain that research does not support the concept of anticipatory grief. Some claim that although it may occur, it is not necessarily common.

Some seek to put a fine point on it, arguing that whatever grief occurs before a death is related to other losses that may occur, as it is not possible to "grieve" the loss of a person until an actual death.

I disagree. For one thing, it is simply not possible to identify in any meaningful way what is causing a spouse to grieve when her partner has received a terminal diagnosis. Feelings of sadness and crying are two normal reactions to grief. When I experienced these reactions, if someone had asked me whether they were attributable to the impending loss of my husband or the other losses I was experiencing—or even "caregiver stress"—I would have responded, "Are you crazy? It's *everything!*"

For those who are losing their loved ones to progressive brain diseases, it feels as though you **are** grieving the loss of your spouse.

"The man I married is gone," one woman said to me, describing the husband whose brain tumors left him unable to do anything but sit in a chair and watch television. "He's very polite and nice and he never gets angry and he always says thank you but he's not my husband anymore." After several years she had learned to exist in this in-between land of not feeling married yet not being a widow. She loved her husband and felt bad about feeling the way she did, so she rarely shared her ambivalence towards him with anyone.

The University of Indianapolis asked more than 400 caregivers of individuals with dementia about their biggest barrier as a caregiver. More than 80 percent said it was the loss of the person they used to know.[4]

It is widely termed "ambiguous loss," interacting with someone who's not fully present socially or psychologically.

My husband did not have dementia; however, glioblastoma did cause cognitive changes.

In an earlier book, I wrote extensively about this wonderful man who was truly "one in a million," admired by everyone for his affable nature, wisdom, and integrity. My husband did not lose those qualities, thankfully, but brain cancer affected him in other ways that left me feeling a profound sense of loss.

The experts may dispute whether or not anticipatory grief exists or whether or not it is a semantically correct term, but I was relieved to finally be able to name the chronically distraught state I had experienced as I said goodbye to my husband four hundred fifty-four days in a row.

I think of that period of time as Year Zero of my widowhood. Sort of like Ground Zero. It's where my grief began.

Looking back, I believe I would have been immensely helped by the following as I battled anticipatory grief:

- One-on-one grief counseling.

- A "caregiver advocate" – someone who would have taken on the task of finding resources for me and helping me connect to community services while I focused on caregiving, the increasing amount of day-to-day responsibilities, and dealing with my grief. (Anticipatory grief and caregiving are like peanut butter and jelly; they often—though not always—go together.)

- Friends and family who would have been willing to let me share my grief and fear over an unimaginable diagnosis, who would have allowed me to be less than "strong."

- A support group specifically for those dealing with anticipatory grief.

- A clear understanding of the advantages and disadvantages of palliative care, hospice care, and hospitalization during the final stages of a life-limiting illness.

The times when these situations did occur—the hug from my stepson when I finally broke down a few weeks before my husband's death, the phone calls made by a friend on my behalf during one crisis—stand out in my mind.

The State of Anticipatory Grief is an awful place for a wife to live, but I dreaded the day I would be forced to leave it and travel—no longer a wife but a widow—to my next destination. Despite what I'd been led to believe, dwelling for a while in the State of Anticipatory Grief did nothing to prevent the shock of having my plane crash-land in the State of Normal Grief.

CROSSING OVER
(An essay written in Year One)

Near the end of one of my favorite movies, Thelma and Louise, the doomed duo is driving through the desert, heading towards the Grand Canyon. Thelma turns to her friend and tells her she can't go back because something has "crossed over" in her.

Widowhood is like that.

It feels as if something has "crossed over" in me. Losing my husband to brain cancer has profoundly changed me in ways I am still discovering, day by day. It has also given me a deep sense of separation from those who have not been widowed. It's like being in jail, on the prisoner's side of the plexiglass partition separating me from my visitors. We can each press our hands against the plexiglass, but we are unable to truly connect anymore.

My visitors want me to rejoin them on their side of the partition as soon as possible.

I'm not sure that's going to happen.

I didn't feel this way when I lost other loved ones. Although saddened, I did not feel separated from the "normal" world. This is different, and it feels permanent. Is it because the loved one I lost this time was my husband, or is it because the devastating battle with a progressive, destructive brain disease—something comparatively few people experience—caused me to feel separated from the world long before he died? There is no way to parse it out.

Of course, widows do not have a corner on the market when it comes to tragedy. There are many others on this side of the plexiglass partition. What separates us from the rest of the world? The magnitude of the loss in our own lives, I believe, whatever that loss is. For me, it was my husband.

Those on the other side of the partition have yet to be betrayed by the illusion of forever.

Obviously, I would love to be untouched by widowhood, unable to fully comprehend how it turns your life upside down, shakes you like a rag doll, and leaves you with this searing sense of separation. But I can't turn back time. I can only turn around and join all those who have crossed over before me, many of whom have built new lives for themselves—and even reclaimed a bit of joy. Joy tinged with sadness, I imagine, but joy nonetheless.

Thelma had the right idea about not going back, but I have no intention of soaring off a cliff. I have far too much to do.

NORMAL GRIEF

After I had been widowed for about three years, an acquaintance lost her husband. "At first I was just numb," she said. "Now I'm feeling sad one minute, angry the next… is this normal?"

"Yes," I assured her. "I don't believe in telling other widows what they're going to feel, but I will tell you that there are literally dozens of reactions to grief that are considered perfectly normal."

I told her I had experienced many of them, and most of the widows I knew had, too.

The grief experts may describe these reactions slightly differently, but they appear to be in general agreement that the feelings and behaviors listed below are elements of "normal grief":

- Shock
- Numbness
- Disbelief
- Sadness
- Depression
- Anxiety
- Guilt
- Irritability

- A sense of unreality
- Anger
- Self-reproach
- Fear
- Hysteria
- Helplessness
- Vulnerability
- Loneliness
- Relief
- Mood swings
- Feelings of being crazy
- Absent-mindedness
- Insomnia
- Change in appetite
- Social withdrawal
- Restlessness
- Crying
- Sighing
- Dreaming about, seeing, or hearing the deceased person
- Hallucinations
- Longing or yearning for the deceased
- Inability to focus or make decisions
- Confusion
- Loss of interest in life
- Oversensitivity
- Tightness in chest and throat
- Dizziness
- Headaches
- Weakness
- Fatigue
- Stomach upset
- Pounding heart
- Isolation from or, conversely, overdependence on others

- Self-absorption
- Searching for meaning
- Questioning spiritual beliefs, values, and priorities

As a widow, contemplating the stark black letters on the white page, the succinct adjectives and verbs that have been compiled by the experts, I noted the woeful limitations of language in capturing the widow experience.

And so much was missing from this list.

What about *sheer horror?* I wondered as I thought about the overwhelming feeling that served as the backdrop for all of the above for a very long time.

Oh my God, how did this become my life?

That question was never far from my mind during "normal" grief, and based on my conversations with other widows, that's the form that "disbelief" often takes (rather than disbelief that the husband is dead, although sometimes that can take place, too).

What about *feeling that one's brain has been taken hostage... by the deceased?*

Because for the longest time, it can seem as if every conversation, every action, every glance at every object, every minute of every day, evokes memories of the husband who died.

The inadequacy of a matter-of-fact list of possible responses in describing a widow's experience is doubtless the reason so many metaphors and similes exist about grief (i.e., grief is "like a wave" that comes and goes).

As reflected in my essays and poems, I, too, searched for more meaningful ways to convey my feelings of grief. When I finished writing my first poem ("A Ghost Walking Backwards," written in the final weeks of my husband's life), I realized the advantage of imagery over adjectives in painting a picture of my loss.

I also realized that every time I could capture a bit of it in writing, grief's firm hold on me seemed to loosen slightly.

Normal grief, the experts say, occurs in the vast majority of grievers. The inadequacy of defining it, however, is acknowledged. In *Handbook of Bereavement: Theory, Research and Intervention*, psychiatrists Stephen R. Shuchter and Sidney Zisook pointed out the wide variety of responses to grief, writing that "... attempts to limit its scope or demarcate its boundaries by arbitrarily defining normal grief are bound to fail."[1]

Just when I thought I had read about all the reactions to grief that were considered normal, I would pick up another book and come across another one. *Oh, yeah, I've done that, too.* In his book, *Grief Counseling and Grief Therapy*, psychologist J. William Worden included the phenomenon of carrying around objects that belonged to the deceased.[2] My husband carried a fresh cotton handkerchief with him every day. For months after he died, I carried one of his handkerchiefs in my purse, neatly folded and never to be used. The handkerchiefs had additional personal meaning as I always gave him new ones (in a variety of colors) at Christmas.

One aspect of normal grief that doesn't seem to garner enough attention is the toll it takes physically on the bereaved. At one grief workshop I learned that the immune system can be compromised for at least one year after the death of the loved one. There are many excellent books and articles that go into detail about physiology and widowhood. Bereavement is associated with changes in cortisol response, immune imbalance, altered sleep, and inflammatory cell mobilization, as well as changes in heart rate and blood pressure. These changes are invisible to those around us.

I'm not sure many people understand how profoundly the shock of seeing the person you love after they have passed away can affect a widow physically. Even though my husband's death was expected, five years after the fact I still feel nauseated and sometimes even dizzy when I recall the moment I beheld his lifeless body. It was as if part of me literally died at that moment, too. I can only imagine how traumatic the experience must be for a widow who witnesses her husband's sudden, unexpected death.

It's an understatement to say that it might take a long time for the brain to process the information that the person you lay next to every night, the person you were intimate with, no longer exists in human form. It's not a question of disbelief on an intellectual level; it's just an awful lot to process—too much, really.

Most widows I have known understand that normal grief can include any of the reactions listed at the beginning of this chapter, but what doesn't seem to be so well understood is that normal grief also includes *not* having the vast majority of these responses.

In a widows' social group, I met a woman in her early sixties who had lost her husband to cancer. For over a year we met periodically for lunch, and at one point she confessed, "I'm starting to wonder if something is wrong with me. At our social hours, I listen to all the other widows talking about their feelings and everything they're struggling with… but I feel okay. Ken was able to do quite a bit until the end, so I feel lucky that way. Since he's been gone, I haven't really broken down or anything… just moments of sadness… It's been over a year now and I honestly feel fine."

Over the course of our brief friendship, she never did have a breakdown or a sudden onset of grief. Her personality was simply different from most of the widows I knew. She adjusted to her new life without her husband with seemingly little difficulty.

For her, it was a normal reaction to grief.

She didn't mind talking about her husband's death; she just didn't share my experience or that of most of the widows I met over the years.

What about talking about one's grief? Is it normal? Is *not* talking about it normal? Will not talking about it cause problems later on in life?

I didn't even realize one of my acquaintances was a widow until my own husband died. She had lost her husband in an accident ten years earlier and—since our casual conversations had always been on other subjects—she had simply never mentioned it.

After I became a widow, we went out to lunch. She told me that she had attended one grief support meeting and had not found it helpful. "I couldn't identify with the women and I didn't really feel comfortable talking about my husband's death," she said. "I dealt with it on my own."

She shared that at times she felt sad when she saw couples sitting together in a restaurant, for example, or holding hands, but she certainly didn't seem as if she was suppressing or holding on to unprocessed grief.

I have two elderly relatives by marriage who rarely talk about their late husbands. Even early on, this was the case. They have always believed in "keeping private things private" in all aspects of their lives, and they carried these convictions into widowhood.

Some grief experts have pointed to the fact that there is simply no research to support the common assumption that talking about or processing one's loss is necessary for grievers.[3]

I was confused. It was common knowledge, wasn't it, that one needed to "share" one's grief with someone—if not a group, then family or friends—and not "bottle it up" inside? Based on my personal experience, "sharing" had been helpful. I had just assumed that those who did not do the same would have more difficulties—if not now, at some later point in their life—as a result of not talking about or otherwise processing their grief.

I found that this misconception was widespread among the widows I met over the years. And not just among the widows—even among a few support group facilitators, who warned of the dire consequences in store for those who kept their own counsel and did not share their grief.

So not having the common "reactions" to grief could be perfectly normal, and not talking about grief could be perfectly normal, and even not "processing" one's grief could be considered normal?

It flew in the face of everything that I had heard about grief.

Where I and many others have been mistaken is in assuming that those who are simply grieving without experiencing many reactions or discussing it with their families are the same as those who are avoiding or denying grief altogether. "Absent grief" is an example of grief that is not normal and has specific symptoms that a professional should assess. According to psychologists Margaret Stroebe and Henk Shut, "There is supportive evidence that it may be impossible to avoid grieving unremittingly without severe costs to mental and physical well-being."[4]

I have heard many criticisms over the years from grieving individuals that certain members of their families were "in denial." How many, I couldn't help but wonder, were simply grieving in a "normal" fashion that didn't include the need to talk about their loss? It's so tempting to speak authoritatively about the way others grieve, especially once we experience our own deep grief. We understand on an intellectual level that not everyone is going to grieve for our husbands the way we do, but do we really understand at a gut level how different that grieving process might be?

What about the issue of time as it relates to normal grief?

Because if I could add yet another response to the list of normal reactions to widowhood, I would include *Yearning for a grief timeline.*

A woman is pregnant for nine months. Children go to school for twelve years. Seasons last precisely three months. We like to know when things—especially things we don't like—are going to end.

In their article, "The Course of Normal Grief," Schucter and Zisook noted that when it comes to normal grief, "...the expected time course... has increased through the years." (This was in comparison to the early grief experts' conclusions that grieving took mere weeks or months.)[5]

I've read articles by grief experts who claim normal grief lasts about a year. Others say at least two years. That is not to say that grieving does not continue in some manner for years to come, but that for the majority it is no longer acute.

Some experts simply say there is no timetable. Period. As is the case with certain other aspects of grief, theories vary. It can take a long time for a widow to realize that the yearning for a time frame can't be satisfied, and that there will be no definitive "end point."

In my opinion it really doesn't matter what number of months or years is attached to grief, because when my husband died, time lost much of its meaning. It was as if a part of me splintered off and was frozen in time and in place, turned into a pillar of salt like Lot's wife. My husband was in my life for twenty years, but all those years blurred together into a timeless "other life."

"How long has your husband been gone?" When someone learns I'm a widow, that's the first question they ask. I'm sometimes tempted to reply, "Why ask me that? You must think it will tell you something about me, because you will automatically make a judgment – *oh, five years, she must be recovered by now* – but it will tell you nothing. Some days five years is yesterday and some days five years is a lifetime ago. And what do you mean by 'gone'? He was just here an hour ago, whispering, 'Way to go, babe,' in my ear when I finished doing my taxes by myself."

But of course I never say any such thing. I answer politely, and occasionally I'm startled into humility and gratitude when the response is perceptive. *"It can be hard for such a long time, can't it?"*

Five years after my husband's death, in spite of having adapted well to my new circumstances, I continue to feel as if I live in a world where time as expressed by years since his death has little meaning.

Instead, I think of time as expressed by where I have lived and am currently living in Grief Country. But how do you explain that to someone? "I no longer dwell in the State of Complicated Grief but I'm still living in Grief Country. I haven't been to the State of Depression in a few years, but I just spent a week in the State of Sadness because last month was the anniversary of our first date, our wedding, and his death."

It's natural to ask the question, "How long has it been?" and I occasionally do it myself, but I think of it as similar to the generic greeting (unrelated to grief), "How are you?"—a largely rhetorical and meaningless question.

The umbrella of normal grief is so vast, covering such a wide array of reactions, methods of intellectual processing, and styles of grieving, that it covers most of Grief Country.

The experts seem to be in agreement that the majority of grievers (perhaps 85 to 90 percent) experience normal grief.

Historically, however, they have not always been in agreement about the nature and course of grief, as I soon discovered.

ONE HUNDRED YEARS OF GRIEF

I felt my irritation mount as I listened to the "expert" addressing the afternoon talk show host. "There are five stages of grief," she said, alternating her remarks between the host and another guest, a grieving mother. "Denial, anger, bargaining, depression, acceptance..."

"You don't know what you're talking about!" I said indignantly to the well-meaning counselor on my television screen. "Haven't you read a single book about grief in the past four decades?"

The talk show host was nodding sagely and the "expert" was still speaking, but that one sentence had been enough for me and I turned off the television set.

I was certainly no grief expert—in fact, I had probably acquired just enough knowledge to be dangerous—but even I knew the "five stages of grief" theory made famous by Elisabeth Kübler-Ross in the 1960s had been discredited many years ago. It turned out that Kübler-Ross had developed her "stage theory" not for the bereaved but for those who were terminally ill (based on open-ended case studies). Her theory was adapted to those who were grieving the loss of a loved one, even though Kübler-Ross had conducted no valid research of bereaved individuals. Her 1969 book, *On Death and Dying*, was a best-seller, and the "five stages of grief" theory quickly gained popularity, becoming firmly embedded in the national psyche.

Stages, models, tasks, processes, phases, trajectories… Over the years the grief experts have described their theories regarding bereavement as such, with accompanying numbers ranging from two to ten. (I was struck by the experts' fondness for numerical lists.)

As I jotted down details of theory after theory, a vision sprang to mind: the cover of a magazine at the supermarket checkout counter: *Complete the 5 Tasks of Grief by Summer! . . . Are You Resilient? Take Our New Quiz! . . . 25 Symptoms of Normal Grief! . . . 2 Types of Grievers Recently Identified! . . . One Widow's Success Story Using 4 Phases Theory!*

Setting aside irreverent widow humor, however, I attempted to make some sense of what I was reading about a few of the grief theories developed over the past one hundred years. While a few sentences written by a layperson obviously cannot do justice to the many years of work by these experts, they may provide a simple historical framework.

1917 – Grief Work

In 1917 Sigmund Freud (commonly regarded as the founder of psychoanalysis) wrote an essay entitled, "Mourning and Melancholia." He differentiated "mourning," which involved the ego detaching from the deceased, from "melancholia," which was an unhealthy attachment (grief "of a morbid pathological disposition").

Freud introduced the idea of *"**grief work**."* Grief work involved the aforementioned **detachment**, plus **readjustment** and **development of new relationships**. According to Freud, this work should be accomplished as quickly as possible. He wrote, "When the work of mourning is completed the ego becomes free and uninhibited again."[1]

1944 – First Study of Grief; Anticipatory Grief

In 1944 Harvard psychiatrist Erich Lindemann wrote "The Symptomology and Management of Acute Grief." Like Freud, he believed "grief work" (dealing head-on with the death and adjusting to a new reality) was necessary. His study of 101 individuals who had lost loved ones under traumatic circumstances was the first empirical study of grief. Lindemann also coined the term, "anticipatory grief."[2]

1960s to 1980s - Phases and Stages

In the 1960s (and 1970s) psychologist John Bowlby applied his infant **attachment theory** (which described the reactions an infant or child has when his or her mother is taken away) to the loss of a loved one. Some of the reactions, such as anger and sadness, have been borne out to be normal reactions to grief, albeit not experienced in a linear fashion.

During the same time period, psychiatrist Colin Murray Parkes was developing a theory that grief was characterized by alarm; searching; mitigation; anger and guilt; and gaining a new identity.[3]

In 1980 Bowlby and Parkes joined together to develop the *"**four phases**"* theory. Their phases were 1) shock and numbness; 2) yearning and searching; 3) disorganization and despair; and 4) reorganization.[4]

In 1969 Elisabeth Kübler-Ross offered her theory about grief's *"five stages"*: 1) denial, 2) anger, 3) bargaining, 4) depression, and 4) acceptance.[5]

In the 1980s psychologist J. William Worden introduced the idea that grief is *a process,* not a state, with *four tasks* of mourning: to accept the reality of loss; to experience the pain of grief; to adjust to an environment in which the deceased is missing, and to withdraw emotional energy and invest it in another relationship.[6]

Worden subsequently updated the wording of the fourth task to "emotionally relocate the deceased and move on with life," then updated it again to "find an enduring connection with the deceased while embarking on a new life." These changes reflected the change in thinking that was to take place among experts about whether or not "letting go" was required in the way Freud had stated.

1990s – Processes; Meaning; Rethinking Old Theories

In 1993 Therese A. Rando, Ph.D., said there were *three phases* of grief and mourning: the avoidance phase, the confrontation phase, and the accommodation phase.[7] She also presented the *"six R processes"* of grief: recognize the death, react, recollect, reorganize, relinquish, readjust, and reinvest.[8]

In 1996 Thomas Attig, Ph.D., refuted the ideas of *"stages or phases"* of grief and the *assumption that grieving ends* when we complete stages or "recover"; and he also emphasized the *individuality* of grieving.[9]

In 1996 Dennis Klass said it was healthy to *continue a bond* with the deceased.[10] As mentioned, this was a change from the earlier recommendations that a loved one needed to "let go" of the person.

In the late 1990s Robert Neimeyer developed his model of *meaning reconstruction* (making sense of life, finding benefits, reconstructing the loss).[11]

In 1999 psychologists Margaret Stroebe and Henk Schut introduced a *"dual process"* model. They said the griever had two categories of stressors, one loss-oriented (experiencing emotional reactions) and one restoration-oriented (dealing with secondary sources of stress). The griever was advised to try to alternate (oscillate) between these two categories of stressors. They noted the "additional necessity to take time off from the pain of grief."[12]

2000s – Resilience; Narrative as Meaning

In the early 2000s, Neimeyer emphasized that his model of finding meaning included the importance of encouraging a griever to tell her stories as well as seek new meaning in order to build a new life.[13] Other experts soon joined in on promoting the concept of "finding meaning."

In 2004 George Bonnano wrote "Loss, Trauma, and Human Resilience," describing his "multiple trajectories" theory. He said grievers most often followed one of three paths: "resilience," "recovery," or "chronic grieving."[14]

In 2004 Elisabeth Kübler-Ross co-authored (with David Kessler) *On Grief and Grieving: Finding the Meaning of Grief Through the Five Stages of Loss*, in which she asserted that her five stages theory, made famous after the publication of 1969's *On Death and*

Dying, had been misunderstood and that the stages had never been intended to be applied in a linear fashion.[15] (Kübler-Ross passed away before *On Grief and Grieving* was published in 2005.)

There are more theories that have been put forth—by psychologists, psychiatrists, social workers, and others—but my intention is not to take a deep dive into grief theories. Rather, it is to 1) highlight a few of the theories that appeared most frequently as I read a variety of books; 2) emphasize that the widely known "five stages of grief" theory was put forth in the infancy of the modern grief studies movement; and 3) demonstrate that beliefs about the nature and course of grief seem to change every few years.

The plethora of theories, some conflicting, led me to conclude that there is virtually nothing "official" about the course of grief.

There is no "grief czar" or single, widely recognized, preeminent expert who has deconstructed the experience of grief to the universal satisfaction of the bereaved, fellow grief experts, and the general public.

It is interesting to note that some of the synonyms for "theory" as used by the general public are hypothesis, conjecture, supposition, assumption, and speculation. In science, "theory" is linked with observation. Researchers organize their observations of individuals and link them to a principle to form a theory. Although research methods have certainly become more fine-tuned (as discussed further in the chapter entitled, "Research Has Shown..."), the theories developed from research are by definition not set in stone.

Last year I "binge-watched" a television series that was popular a few years ago called *The Good Wife*. The protagonist, a defense attorney, often came up against a quirky judge who insisted that any declarative statements made by defense attorneys and prosecutors alike must be followed by the phrase, "in my opinion."

After watching the TV show, a little voice inside my head automatically began whispering, *"in your opinion"* every time I read about a different theory of grief.

The grief constructs developed by the experts extend beyond putting forth theories. In this book I use the designations of "normal grief," "complicated grief," etc., but even those designations are merely categories that have been created and used by the experts over the years.

2017—Approaching Consensus

When my head stopped spinning from trying to absorb everything I was reading, my overall impression was that 1) a consensus had been reached by most experts that the old "stage" and "phase" theories (defining grief in a linear fashion) had been nearly universally debunked and/or discarded; 2) many of the other models of grief had useful components; 3) the differences in processing grief are exceedingly widespread; 4) research methods have improved over the years; and 5) most people will eventually come to terms with their grief in a "normal" fashion no matter what they do.

During the six months immediately following my husband's death, I was caring for my mother, so none of the theories about grief or recommended "tasks" related to healing had any significance. I was virtually frozen in time, just trying to survive the day at hand.

After my mother moved to a care facility, however, I found myself instinctively following the "dual process" model of grief espoused by Stroebe and Shut. At the time I was unaware of their theories and the extensive research they had performed.

As stated earlier, the dual process model suggests the griever switch between "loss-oriented" activities and "restoration-oriented" activities. From what I observed of my widowed friends over the years, many of them were already instinctively following this model, too, allowing themselves to experience the *ruminating, despair, and emotional aspects* of widowhood for a time before switching back to the task of *dealing with all the adjustments* necessitated by their loss.

Another one of the experts' theories struck a distinct chord with me. I began writing a memoir after my husband died, and upon finishing the first draft, I read about the importance of telling one's stories (narrative as an element of Robert Neimeyer's "meaning reconstruction" theory) in order to make sense of the past, present, and future. Widowhood and its aftermath had made telling my story imperative for me, but I had no idea at the time that the urgency I felt about making sense of my life—from traumas in childhood to devastating losses as an adult—might be in line with a grief expert's theory.

The theories that resonated the most with me were Stroebe and Shut's "dual process" theory and Neimeyer's "meaning reconstruction" theory. I also found George Bonanno's "trajectories of grief" research illuminating (as discussed in the chapter entitled "Resilience and Rebuilding").

If one types the word "grief" into Amazon's Book Department search engine, more than 40,000 titles will be retrieved. Most were published after Elisabeth Kübler-Ross popularized the subject of grief in 1969. One might think the subject would be exhausted by now, after nearly fifty years, but that is not the case.

Why do we continue to explore the subject of grief so assiduously? Perhaps because it is as all-encompassing yet as elusive as the subject of love, and goodness knows, we are obsessed with love. Experts divide grief "symptoms" into categories (such as cognitive, social, emotional, physical, behavioral, and feelings), but the same categories could apply to love.

Grief and love are like puzzles we will never be able to finish because we will never have all the jigsaw pieces. The variables are endless.

After researching the major grief theories, it certainly seems possible that today's "new understanding" of grief may become tomorrow's "discarded theory." *In my opinion!*

Since the time of Sigmund Freud's exploration of grief, exactly one hundred years ago, the experts have been roaming around Grief Country, tracing and analyzing the journeys of the bereaved. Like us widows, sometimes they compare notes on their travels.

I could never hope to acquire all the knowledge of those who devote their lives to the study of grief. It's fascinating to study their theories and gain insights, but so far, the experts haven't been able to provide the one thing that widows really want from them—an escape route that will lead us out of Grief Country.

Blue sky promises

broken into drops of rain—

I still miss you so

(Haiku for Ron written on Valentine's Day,
Year Two)

~~COMPLICATED GRIEF~~
WHEN GRIEF IS NOT "NORMAL"

No, this chapter title does not reflect a proofreading error.

So why would I strike through the term, "complicated grief?"

Because as I studied grief, I became increasingly confused by the references to grief reactions that are not considered normal. The nomenclature keeps changing!

Complicated grief has also been called "prolonged grief," "chronic grief," and "persistent complex bereavement disorder." As I discovered with other definitions, the exact definition of complicated grief varies among those who study grief. It has been described in some materials as an intense, lingering, or extreme reaction to loss and in others as a sort of umbrella term that covers a host of specific, abnormal reactions to loss.

For purposes of this chapter, I am using "complicated grief" as an umbrella term.

Here are some variations of complicated grief that appeared in the books I read:

Delayed grief

Prolonged or *chronic grief*

Absent grief (aka *masked, inhibited,* or *repressed grief*)

Distorted grief (aka *exaggerated grief*)

Excessive grief

Unresolved grief (aka *layered grief*)

Concomitant grief

Trauma-related grief

Some of these types of grief have more than one name, and the experts have different opinions about their definitions and nature. It's not my intention, since I am not an expert, to go into detail about each of these complicated grief reactions, but as I looked back upon my own experience, I did come to the conclusion that I had experienced complicated grief.

During the time my husband was dying from glioblastoma multiforme (grade four brain cancer), I was also spending much of my time caring for my mother, who was suffering from Alzheimer's disease as well as chronic mental health issues (including schizophrenia).

Two months after I became a widow, my mother was found wandering on the freeway and my caregiving responsibility for her instantly changed from part time to full time.

My mother's needs were extensive, and it soon became clear that my bereavement was going to have to take a back seat to her care. She lived in my home, needed my assistance for nearly all activities of daily living, and she could not be left alone for her own safety. In addition, her emotional health was extremely fragile.

My grief had to be put on hold.

In fact, for a number of months I had to pretend, for my mother's sake, that I never had a husband who died. I had many photographs on display in my house that included him, but Alzheimer's was quickly robbing her of the ability to recognize anyone from pictures. I mentioned him rarely and eventually, not at all, as it became obvious that she no longer remembered him.

Day in and day out, for close to six months, I could not allow myself to cry except for ten minutes in the shower or during a 90-minute support group once a month. I could not leave my mother alone and excuse myself to have a mini-breakdown. Any time I was fortunate enough to have someone else care for her was time that had to be spent grocery shopping, running errands, etc. I had to stuff my grief into a deep, dark hole.

I was definitely not able to experience normal grief at that time.

When my mother eventually moved to an adult family home with 24-hour supervision, I was finally able to begin the process of grieving my husband.

Did I experience a form of complicated grief called *delayed grief*? According to the experts, delayed grief is usually accompanied by intense emotions and, quite often, depression. Both were true for me.

(It should be noted that there are some experts who do not believe delayed grief exists, just as there are those who do not believe anticipatory grief exists.)

I also believe I was experiencing *concomitant grief*, which is characterized by several significant losses occurring simultaneously or in close succession. No sooner had my husband died than I was plunged right back into the anticipatory grief and ambiguous loss that accompanies an Alzheimer's diagnosis. For all intents and purposes, I was losing—or had already lost—my mother, too. Factoring in all the other losses I was experiencing, it was indeed overwhelming.

That was one reason it was important for me to learn about complicated grief. As mentioned earlier, I suspected my grief journey was not following the course of "normal grief."

Another reason I wanted to learn about complicated grief was prompted by my frustration upon hearing people—even fellow widows—make declarative statements about grief that did not take into account the unique circumstances and challenges of individual widows.

At a small gathering of widows, I witnessed one woman telling another widow, "If *I* could do it, *you* can do it. We've *all* gone through the same thing." She seemed to be a bit impatient with the second widow's unchecked tears as she lamented what a hard time she was having.

The first widow probably intended to be encouraging in a "tough love" kind of way, but her statement that we had all gone through the same thing was incorrect. The second widow had lost both her parents along with her husband within a very short time frame. Significant losses in short succession. It sounded like *concomitant grief* to me.

The adage, "Everyone grieves differently," is ubiquitous, but perhaps the adage should actually be, "Everyone grieves differently, in accordance with a vast array of unique circumstances."

And some of those unique circumstances may contribute to the likelihood that grief will not be "normal," but "complicated." How is a widow to know if she is experiencing complicated grief? In addition to consulting a trained and licensed professional, there are assessment tools available, as described later in this chapter.

Different experts cite different statistics, but in general somewhere between 10 to 15 percent of people experience complicated grief. It occurs more often in women—particularly older women—than men.

Widows have a greater risk of complicated grief if they lost their spouse from a sudden, unexpected event or trauma. A preexisting history of depression can also be a factor. Those did not apply to me, but other risk factors did: a highly dependent relationship with my late husband, social isolation, loss of support/friends, and even an abusive and/or traumatic childhood. (I had no idea an abusive childhood could be a factor in grieving.)

Complicated grief may change the course of bereavement for a widow, but is it a mental disorder?

Health care professionals use a handbook published by the American Psychiatric Association, entitled The Diagnostic and Statistical Manual of Mental Disorders (DSM), for diagnosing mental disorders, such as major depressive disorder.

Until recently, those who were grieving could not be diagnosed with major depressive disorder. It was called the "bereavement exclusion."

Now, however, that exclusion has been eliminated (in the DSM-5). A person who meets all the criteria for major depressive disorder will no longer be denied that diagnosis just because the person recently lost a loved one.

This is a change of potentially great significance for grievers, as the cost of treatment must be covered by health insurance if that insurance policy covers major depressive disorder treatment for non-grievers.

The DSM-5 notes that "In distinguishing grief from a major depressive episode (MDE), it is useful to consider that in grief the predominant affect is feelings of emptiness and loss, while in MDE it is persistent depressed mood and the inability to anticipate happiness or pleasure."[1]

A widow who suspects she is suffering from a major depressive disorder should be diagnosed by a professional psychologist, psychiatrist, or other duly licensed health care professional who can provide appropriate treatment.

When I was struggling with my grief, I did not know there was such a thing as a Grief Intensity Scale. This method for assessing grief reactions was developed by Holly G. Prigerson and Paul K. Maciejewski of Weill Cornell Medical College and is one method to determine whether a widow is experiencing grief that is not normal. It is available online. [2]

Additional assessment tools are listed in the chapter entitled, "Research Has Shown..."

Disenfranchised Grief

Although it doesn't fall under the umbrella of "complicated grief," there is another type of grief that widows might want to consider: *disenfranchised grief.* This concept was introduced in 1989 by Kenneth J. Doka, Ph.D.[3]

Disenfranchised grief (also known as hidden grief) is grief that may not be acknowledged by society for a variety of reasons, and it can apply to different types of losses. As it relates to widowhood, perhaps the husband died by suicide or other means that typically carries a stigma, or family members don't want to acknowledge a same-sex marriage or committed relationship existed. Sometimes disenfranchised grief can be experienced by previous wives.

After my husband died, I came across the ring his ex-wife had given him when they married thirty years earlier. During our own marriage we had shared with each other that we had each kept our rings from our previous spouses. We both felt that the rings were part of our individual histories, nothing more, so no misunderstandings existed.

What should I do with this ring? I wondered. My husband and his ex-wife had been married a relatively short time (about six years) but they had co-parented their children for another decade or so. They had not been in contact for a number of years prior to my husband's death.

As I considered what to do, I recalled that a few years earlier, one of my relatives had told me how upset she had been upon hearing that her ex-husband died, even though she hadn't seen him for more than a decade, their marriage had been very unhappy, and she had always been highly critical of him. It made no sense to me at the time, but reading about disenfranchised grief helped me to understand my relative's perspective better than I had at the time.

I made a decision. I placed my husband's ring from his first marriage in a small box and attached a note. *"I thought you might want to have this back. Stephanie"*

I kept the note simple, just a sentence. I then sent it to my stepdaughter to give to her mother. It cost me nothing to acknowledge whatever grief she might be feeling.

The State of Feeling Disenfranchised is a part of Grief Country that may not be as large as other states, like the State of Sadness, but it attracts its share of visitors, nonetheless.

Complicated grief wends its way through many of the states in Grief Country, such as the State of Post-Traumatic Stress Disorder, the State of Social Isolation, and the State of Cumulative Losses.

The main point I want to make about complicated grief (or grief that is not "normal") is that people—not just widows but their friends and loved ones—need to understand that it exists. Once people understand that personal histories and unique circumstances may factor into why Jane or Mary or Linda "just can't seem to get over it" as quickly as another widow might, perhaps there will be less judgment and more support for these widows.

HAUNTED
(Written in Year Two)

You're not a shining star in the sky
a gentle spirit carried on the breeze
my own special angel
or any of the things they say
in their beautiful poetry
designed to console
the inconsolable

You appear without warning
whispering sweet words of remembrance
caressing my tear-stained cheek
before you fade away
I wait with eagerness
and dread
for your return

Why did you leave me
if you still refuse to leave me?
You come and go at will
My shattered heart remains your home
There's nothing more cruel
than loving someone as perfectly
as you loved me

ANGER

It's the dirty little secret of widowhood.

Anger.

Behind our carefully composed exteriors, a lot of us are angry. Angry that we lost our husbands, angry that our hopes and dreams have been swept away, angry that we have to start over, and angry at the people around us who have either backed away from our grief or judged how we are dealing with it.

Many of us are even angry with our husbands for dying. I wrote "Haunted" because I was angry that my husband kept coming back to me in dreams. (When the dreams subsided, I then became angry with myself for driving him away by writing the poem.)

Anger is one of the "normal" reactions to grief. Not every widow experiences it. Most of the widows I know, however, have struggled with it to varying degrees.

We conceal it well. In fact, the unwidowed world usually has nary a clue as to just how incensed we really are. Every widow quickly learns that in Grief Country, a display of anger is a one-way ticket to the State of The Uninvited.

So the anger simmers beneath the surface, bubbling up periodically when we are in the company of other widows.

Other times, it bursts forth in inappropriate ways.

I remember the day I vented my anger at a neighbor. I had been widowed for three months and had taken my mother into my home as advancing Alzheimer's made it impossible for her to live on her own.

One day I took my eyes off my mother for a short time and she opened the front door, allowing my two small dogs to run outside into the street. An older man was taking his daily walk and my dogs began barking at him furiously. I quickly scooped up my Chihuahua but my toy poodle eluded my grasp, running circles around the man, still barking and trying to appear menacing.

The man kept walking briskly, ignoring the chaos around him. I kept calling my dog's name and attempting to corral him, unsuccessfully. This ridiculous parade of barking and chasing and striding continued down the block for several minutes.

Just then another neighbor's medium-sized dog ran over and began barking, too. Seeing the larger dog, my toy poodle lost his courage and suddenly decided to allow me to pick him up, too. As I struggled to hold my two dogs in my arms, the medium-sized dog then began to jump up and nip at my toy poodle's bottom.

The fellow taking his morning walk turned towards me and, without breaking stride, angrily snapped, "You're supposed to keep your dogs on a leash, you know!"

"Look, I'm *sorry!*" I retorted in a raised voice as frustration and anger gripped me. "My husband just died and my mother has Alzheimer's and she let the dogs out and I *do* put leashes on them when I take them out, so why don't you just *give me a break*, for God's sake!"

With that I turned heel and hustled home, hoping my mother hadn't gotten into any mischief in the few minutes I'd been away.

I was so angry. Angry at my neighbor but also angry that God had allowed my surly neighbor to live and let my husband die. My husband would *never* have kept walking, much less scolded a lady in distress. He would have stopped and gallantly helped her gain control of the situation.

For a long time it felt as if I was living with a stab wound that would not close. When someone made careless or unthinking comments, I wanted to scream in anger, "Stop *hurting* me! What's wrong with you? Can't you see I'm still *bleeding?*"

Like a blazing inferno, a widow's pain can be so all-consuming that it seems impossible that others do not feel the heat. And when it becomes obvious that they don't, it can make us angry.

There were times early on when I shared my anger with a friend with whom I felt I could be honest. She let me be angry, but the situation made her highly uncomfortable. I didn't realize how much until we discussed it years later.

The fact is, anger is arguably the one "normal" reaction to grief that is usually unacceptable.

Anger is viewed by most people as an entirely negative emotion. Psychologists don't necessarily agree. Many see it as an indicator of feelings, thoughts, etc., that need to be explored and dealt with. It can also motivate us to take action. If folks are angered by social injustice, for example, they may find that anger spurs them to band together and right societal wrongs. It's when we lash out at innocent people or when anger becomes excessive and damaging to us physically and mentally that it becomes toxic.

The grief experts agree that anger is a normal reaction to grief and that it may even have value. Psychologist George Bonanno points out that "a bereaved person who feels vulnerable due to the emotional upheaval of grief might use anger to fortify herself for the upcoming struggle."[1]

In their article, "Anger: The Hidden Part of Grief," Mary S. Cerney, Ph.D. and James R. Buskirk, M.D. warn that not recognizing and resolving feelings of anger may interfere with the process of grieving. [2]

Although I don't believe that it's a "stage," the best exposition of anger that I read was from Elisabeth Kübler-Ross's *On Grief and Grieving*, wherein she devotes several pages to the "stage" of anger. "It is important to feel the anger without judging it, without attempting to find meaning in it," she wrote.[3]

The experts encourage finding ways to channel anger, perhaps expressing it through writing or art, or relieving it through exercise. All good information, but what I needed was to be able to *share* my anger. And the only safe place for me to do this was in the company of other widows.

I have attended many support group sessions where I have witnessed this anger spill forth, usually accompanied by the widow's palpable relief at being able to be so brutally honest without fear of judgment.

Expressing my anger and hearing other widows express theirs was like letting the air out of a toxic balloon. At some point, the balloon that has been filled with every suppressed breath of rage simply must be deflated.

I would be remiss if I failed to acknowledge the widows who have told me that they simply "turned their anger over to God." There is no single, "right way" to deal with anger, and everyone's path should be honored.

For most widows the anger usually doesn't persist—at least not to the same degree—as there are too many other places in Grief Country that must be visited. Obviously, if a widow takes up residence in the State of Anger for years, she might need professional help, but what I and most of my widowed friends needed was simply an outlet, the ear of someone with empathy and the willingness to be uncomfortable for a short time.

Someone who would bear with us until we could accept the stark truth that no one has the answer to the angrily posed but essential question of our new lives: *What the hell am I supposed to do with all this pain?*

We live in a society where most people seem to have little difficulty with expressing their anger about a myriad of subjects, ranging from the trivial to the more serious, but at the same time they cannot bring themselves to bear witness to the anger of widows.

So we share our fury with each other and often discover that we no longer become angry about most of the things that routinely incense the unwidowed.

It's ironic. We witness those around us rage and shake their fists about things that often can be ignored or fixed, yet as widows we are not supposed to show anger about our life-altering loss, which can't be ignored or fixed.

So we keep our dirty little secret.

GHOST TOWN
(Written in Year Three)

Chasing memories like tumbleweeds
glancing off boarded-up buildings
Twisted twigs and sand and yesterday
eluding my frantic grasp

Prying off plywood and rusty nails
Reaching for your silhouette
through a broken window
Gaping at the dust in my hand

Our past glitters in a dry creek bed
Shimmering in the noonday sun
Snatched up, held tightly against my chest
I treasure even fools' gold

Fresh-picked rose on barren ground
Nothing more to leave
except my heart, my soul, my promise
I will always come back for you

PART II

COPING

WHO AM I NOW?

After becoming a widow, I spent a great deal of time in the State of Questioning My Identity.

One of the common characteristics of widowhood is "a loss of identity."

At the time my husband was diagnosed with glioblastoma, my primary identity was that of being his wife. My secondary identity revolved around helping a group of Bantu refugees resettle in the United States. In addition to trying to learn their language, I was beginning to write a book about the experiences of my refugee friends (who were preliterate and thus unable to record their own stories).

When my husband and I moved to a different city for his cancer treatment, my mother's care needs, and to be closer to his children, I immediately lost my identity as a respected community volunteer and an advocate for refugees. Language studies and writing quickly fell by the wayside.

My new identity was that of a "caregiver," and I embraced my new identity with a fierce determination to help save my husband's life, or, if that was not possible, to make the rest of his life as happy as I could.

My husband had a wonderful team of physicians, nurses, physical therapists, a hospital social worker, and later in his illness an equally conscientious band of hospice workers. It was heartening to be part of a team, all working towards the same goal, and I was gratified by the respect and acknowledgment of my role that I received.

When he died, the team that had supported my husband through his cancer journey sent a lovely card and moved on, as should be expected.

I was surprised by the sense of loss I felt when I read the card and realized I would never see those people again. Then it struck me that my sense of loss might also be attributed to the fact that the sympathy card represented the official loss of my identity as my husband's caregiver.

Within two months of my husband's death, I became a full-time caregiver again (for my mother). Eventually, however, I was alone once more—for good this time.

I was no longer a wife, no longer a community volunteer, and no longer a full-time caregiver. I had no biological children and no job prospects—in spite of more than twenty-five years of work experience.

In the eyes of the world, I had no value (a feeling that was confirmed by the lack of response to the resumes I sent out). I was not prepared for the depth of the uselessness that now seemed to define me.

Who am I now? Since my husband's death I've spoken with dozens of women who have asked themselves that question. So many of us have had to create new identities at a time in our lives when our still-married peers are confidently making retirement plans with their husbands.

I clearly had a lot of work to do.

I started with addressing the literal question: Who am I?

During my marriage the focus had always been on my husband and his family—their history, their traditions, their stories. They were about as close to a Norman Rockwell family as one could get, and I had a cordial relationship with them.

But they were not my family by blood.

A few years earlier, my uncle had given me copies of some of the genealogy research he had undertaken. One day I decided to locate those files and delve into my ancestry. Wading into the ocean of genealogy was the perfect way to distract myself from my grief for a time. Anyone who pursues genealogy as a hobby knows that it can quickly become addicting and all-consuming. Trying to trace the journey of my third great-grandfather from Ireland to Canada and across the United States translated into an entire day without tears.

I didn't know it at the time, but I was applying an aspect of the model of grief proposed by Margaret Stroebe and Henk Shut. I was "taking a break from grief," as mentioned in an earlier chapter of this book.

From my research I was able to trace the journey of one of my great-grandmothers. She was only a teenager when she traveled by wagon train from Wisconsin to Washington state, where she married my great-grandfather. She gave birth to my grandfather and another son before becoming a widow at age twenty-eight. A few years later she married again, but her second husband died when she was just forty-seven years old. Twice widowed, she remained single the rest of her life. She was buried in a small cemetery in Washington state that boasted it was the "cemetery of pioneers."

My great-grandmother is one of the few ancestors of whom I have a photograph. She was a very stern-looking lady, and I suspect I might have been a bit afraid of her in real life, but I choose to regard her as a role model. She survived widowhood twice, endured much hardship, and her pioneer blood runs through my veins.

I have a few other strong women in my ancestry, including one of my grandmothers, who survived the loss of her infant daughter due to an accident and the wrongful death of her youngest son (my uncle) at the hands of the police. (The case was in the local newspaper headlines for weeks before a settlement was reached.) Like me, my grandmother became a widow in her early fifties.

I realized as I studied my genealogy that many of my female ancestors had been widowed at about my age. I was descended from survivors, strong women who did not let hardship, loss, or grief overpower them.

Knowing this was the first step in reclaiming my identity.

The second step was to remember what my passions had been at the time my husband was diagnosed with glioblastoma and determine whether any of those passions could be part of my new life. Obviously, I could no longer center my life around my marriage. I had also moved far away from the refugees I had helped for many years, so I knew that for the time being, my identity would not be based on my service to a refugee community.

What I could do, however, was try to finish writing the book I had begun years earlier, chronicling the early years of their journey in America.

I could reclaim my identity as a fledgling writer.

The third step was to consider all the reasons my husband had chosen me to be his life partner. I was fortunate to have had a husband who wrote wonderful notes and letters, and one day he had given me a list of "Ten Things I Love About My Wife." I reread that list and realized all the qualities he said I possessed were still present. They were part of my identity, too.

Little by little, I plastered together the broken bricks of my identity and built myself up again. I eventually found a job that restored my identity as someone who could support herself. I found other avenues by which to reclaim my identity as a volunteer.

It took me nearly three years to feel as if I had reestablished my own identity after the death of my husband. It was not easy, by any means, and I often had to call upon a higher power to hoist those broken bricks for me, but in the end I knew who I was to a degree I had never known before.

I never set foot in the State of Questioning My Identity again.

One term used by experts when referring to the loss of identity is "reduced self-clarity." It is an apt description. How can a widow see herself clearly while standing in the thick fog of early widowhood? She squints into the mirror but all she can see is emptiness.

It can take a long time for the fog to lift and the mirror to reflect everything that was inside her all along.

And everything she can still become.

THE 6.5 PERCENT

When I became a widow, I was an anomaly among my peers. Suddenly I realized that I didn't know any other widows my age. It's not that I was young, by any means. I just wasn't as old as most widows.

I discovered that according to the U.S. Census Bureau, in the age range of 50-59, only 6.5 percent of women fell into the category of "ever widowed." (It was 4.9 percent for "currently widowed" women in my age range; however, most widows I know believe "widowed" means "ever widowed.")[1]

I was a member of the age group of widows that's "in between"—no longer young but not yet senior citizens. Middle-aged—but leaning slightly more towards the "aged" than the "middle."

In the five years since my husband's death, I have met many, many widows of all ages, each dealing with a unique set of challenges. I don't think any widow necessarily has it "easier" than any other widow. I've met elderly widows who have struggled to deal with critical financial and health issues and I've also met younger widows trying to raise children on their own, often while working full time.

I can't speak for the elderly or young widows, but in general, the 6.5 percent share many characteristics.

We have lost our husbands just as we were starting to flesh out plans for retirement, just as we were beginning to dream of a life together after working full time, after raising children.

We have lost our husbands just as our children have begun living their adult lives in earnest (sometimes moving far away from us), just as grandchildren are arriving—grandchildren who will never know their grandfather.

We have lost our husbands just as we are entering or dealing with menopause, a difficult transition for many women under the best of circumstances.

We are widowed at an age when our parents are in their 70s and 80s, beginning in many cases to need additional assistance. What do we do when we have a parent who can no longer live on his or her own, while we may facing the necessity of selling our own homes due to our new financial circumstances?

In one of the grief workshops I attended, a facilitator said, "Loss is cumulative. Every loss brings up previous losses." This can be particularly difficult for the 6.5 percent, as we often lose our parents not long after losing our husbands. Watching my mother die in a similar manner to my husband brought his death back to me on a daily basis during that time.

We have lost our husbands at a time when most of our friends are still "couples," so we congratulate them on their silver anniversaries, all the while knowing we will never have that experience. I was asked to "officiate" at a relative's thirty-year vow renewal a year after my husband died—a daunting task that I gamely accomplished, even though I paid an emotional price on the drive home. Married in mid-life, my husband and I hadn't necessarily counted on thirty years but twenty-five had been a distinct possibility, given our parents' life spans. We didn't make it anywhere close to that silver anniversary.

Widows in their fifties are not old enough to qualify for Social Security benefits (unless there are special circumstances such as disability or minor children) or Medicare, but we *are* old enough to be victims of age discrimination when it comes to hiring practices. I had been out of the work force for a few years before my husband died, and I was shocked to discover that I was now virtually unemployable. Decades of work experience and up-to-date computer skills seemed to count for nothing. It took a long time to find a job—and I was so relieved to be offered a position that I shrugged off the fact that there were no benefits. I was fortunate that my husband had a modest life insurance policy that provided a safety net during this difficult time.

As I reflected upon how widowhood affected me as a woman in her fifties, I realized it also brought out my strengths.

By the time I turned fifty, I knew who I was as a person. Even though I struggled after widowhood with the loss of my social "identity" or status, I didn't have any doubts about the content of my character, my belief system, or my abilities. I was not faced with the uncertainty or self-doubt of youth.

As mentioned earlier, as widows in our fifties we have not only lost our husbands, we are also beginning to lose parents, older relatives, or friends. The flip side of seeing more death is that we become acutely aware we have a limited amount of time remaining to enjoy our lives or make a difference in this world. We can laser-focus on what we want to accomplish.

Even though I wanted to share my life experiences through my writing, I hesitated as I had always been a very private person. As a widow in my fifties, though, I started hearing a voice in my head that grew louder and louder: *You know firsthand how fragile life is, you are running out of time, finish your books, ignore your fears, and leave something behind before it's too late.*

By the time I reached my fifties, the question of children had been settled. (I have adult stepchildren.) When considering my future as a widow, I did not need to factor in a desire to have children. I chose to regard the lack of pressure to date, marry, and procreate as a positive factor.

In the beginning I could only see all the complications and roadblocks of being widowed at my age. It took time to realize I could turn my age into an advantage in dealing with this irreversible turn of events.

As one of the 6.5 percent, Grief Country's State of Questioning Priorities and State of Finding Meaning had particular relevance. Over time I developed a greater understanding of what I was experiencing and the reasons for some aspects of my journey through grief as a woman in her fifties.

Intellectual insights, however, didn't take away the challenges of having to rebuild my life.

It was time to set out on a new road in Grief Country.

RESILIENCE AND REBUILDING

As I struggled to make sense of my personal grief experience, I repeatedly came across references to "resilience." According to the experts, widows who possess resilience are better able to cope with their grief than other, less resilient widows.

Like "anticipatory grief," resilience is defined slightly differently by the grief experts and many definitions abound. In general, resilience refers to our ability to adapt to or "bounce back" from stressful, unexpected, tragic, or challenging events in our lives.

I had survived a host of stressful situations in my life, including a traumatic childhood marked by domestic violence and alcohol abuse. Surely I was already resilient? Didn't that mean I would automatically be a "resilient widow"?

Not necessarily.

As I read the experts' opinions about what factors contribute to resilience, I realized that at the point in time when I became a widow, I lacked many of the attributes and/or support systems that enable a widow to be more resilient.

In his book, *Grief Is A Journey*, Dr. Kenneth Doka asserted that among other things, resilient grievers possess "fewer losses or other stressors in their lives" and receive support from "family and friends, in work, in faith communities, or in school."

I perused the list of characteristics enumerated by Dr. Doka and realized that I only possessed two: "good psychological health" and an "optimistic mindset."[1] Of course, even those two characteristics had received a brutal battering during the years of being a caregiver, then a widow, then a caregiver again.

Some things I could not change. I could not suddenly invent a supportive family or erase the impact that an intense, prolonged period of caregiving had had on me. I could not change the fact that I was still caring for a mother with Alzheimer's. I could not change the previous losses I had experienced. And my husband's devastating diagnosis of brain cancer—a disease that had struck without a warning or a known cause—had severely shaken my belief that I had much, if any, "control" over my life, which is another factor in resilience, according to Dr. Doka.[2]

My natural resilience had taken a beating and I clearly needed to rebuild it. But how?

As I perused the internet, the vision of the lifestyle magazines that grace many supermarket checkout aisles filled my mind once again. Should I read the *5 Tips to Build Resilience,* the *8 Strategies for Resilience,* or the *10 Ways to Becoming Resilient?*

What the heck. I read them all, as well as the recommendations contained in a few books.

It was universally agreed that connections with others was vital. I needed community and support.

I set out to make new connections. I signed up for women's social groups, writing groups, and a public speaking group. I drove up to an hour each way through big city traffic to meet perfect strangers.

I had my share of disappointments. There were many awkward conversations, certainly times when I felt spectacularly out of place, and more than one occasion when I wondered why I didn't just stay home and watch Netflix with my dogs.

But I knew I didn't want to be isolated, and I knew no one was going to come knocking on my door. I was temporarily "stuck" in a city where I knew very few people, so the onus was on me.

I volunteered to help teach English to immigrants for several hours, twice a week. I attended church services, searching for a possible faith community.

I served on a committee to raise funds for research into brain cancer, the disease that claimed my husband's life.

These activities did not take place all at once. They were spread out over time, interspersed with trying to find a job, overseeing my mother's care after she moved to an adult family home, and working on more recommendations from the "resilience to-do list."

A number of experts stressed the importance of setting goals and continuing to learn new things.

As I mentioned earlier, before my husband's illness I had begun writing a book about my experiences with a refugee community. It had been set aside for years as I cared for my husband, then my mother. *I have to finish the book*, I reminded myself when I lost my bearings after widowhood. That goal kept me going during times when little else could. Eventually, I finished not only that book but another I had never expected to write—a memoir. Learning more about the craft of writing kept my brain engaged and gave me a focus that I needed.

Some experts mentioned the importance of taking control and becoming more empowered. I was determined to reclaim the feeling that I did indeed have some control over my life. With every tough decision I made (including moving and letting go of unhealthy relationships), I felt more empowered.

Along with the recommendations that centered on outward activities (including health) were recommendations that addressed a widow's inner life.

Self-care through meditation and relaxation, learning how to have fun again, consciously trying to cultivate a positive attitude, and nurturing hope, gratitude, and a sense of perspective were acknowledged to be key aspects of building resilience.

There was one task that gave me pause in the beginning. How could I develop "a more positive view" of myself, as the American Psychological Association recommended?[3]

There are few things as effective as widowhood in diminishing that positive view. A widow may know who she is as a person—as I did—but that doesn't mean she will be able to maintain a positive view of herself once her status as a wife disappears. I never realized until he was gone how much my husband's favorable opinion contributed to my positive view of myself. He had been such an incredibly supportive cheerleader.

Now it was up to me to be my own cheerleader. It took a ton of self-talk, journaling, affirmations, pats on my own back for small accomplishments, and a determination to ignore the voices in my head that told me as a widow, a former and current caregiver, and a "woman of a certain age," I no longer had value.

Many authors have written articles and books about resilience—the subject has become ubiquitous, in fact—but in this chapter I have included the suggestions that I personally found to be most helpful.

There is one individual who is arguably the preeminent expert on the subject of resilience as it relates to grief. Psychologist George Bonanno began studying bereavement more than twenty years ago and discovered through research that resilience was far more common than previously believed.

In 2004 he asserted in an article entitled, "Loss, Trauma, and Human Resilience," that "… resilience… represents a distinct trajectory from that of recovery, that resilience is more common than often believed, and that there are multiple and sometimes unexpected pathways to resilience." He identified the three most common patterns of grief: resilience, recovery, and chronic grief.[4]

I was finally able to confirm what I had suspected—that the path of the resilient griever had not been my path for the first two years of widowhood.

According to Bonanno's research—presented via a graph—"resilient" grievers have a sharp increase in grief symptoms for approximately six months, followed by a gradual settling into a nearly steady line, punctuated by periodic upticks, until about two years.

The "recovery" graph was more reflective of my experience, showing grief symptoms continuing on at an extreme level for about a year and a half, only steadying near the two-year mark. Despite the fact that I had a setback a few months later, overall I identified with the "recovery" pattern of grief, which seemed to take into account the extended time I dealt with concurrent stressors, lack of support, and the other factors previously mentioned.

The third graph traced the grief reactions of "chronic" grievers. Their symptoms spiked sharply and frequently during most of the two years.

I believe I was a naturally resilient person who temporarily lost her resilience. My husband and I had been highly dependent upon each other. He had filled the role of family, friends, church, school, work, and any other type of community support that might otherwise have been there for me as a griever.

It took time to build my resilience again. I am wiser now, so I don't take my resilience for granted or assume that it cannot be knocked out of me once more. I work hard to maintain it by continuing to stay engaged and make connections.

Even when I'd rather be watching Netflix with my dogs.

When I look back at that period of time, I envision monkey bars, the old playground favorite. Each bar represented a step I was taking in rebuilding my life.

Go out and meet new people – grab the monkey bar and swing to the next one — *Walk into that new church* – grab the next bar – *Make a list of goals* – grab the next bar…

It wasn't easy, but I could feel the muscles of resilience strengthening with each swing. There were times I just couldn't reach that next monkey bar, and after two such falls I nearly gave up.

Eventually, though, I reached the last monkey bar and dropped safely onto the solid ground upon which I stand today.

FINDING MY OWN SONG
(An essay written in Year Two)

*O*h, how we loved our little road trips. My husband and I would toss our suitcases in the back of our van and set out to explore the western United States (we were saving the rest of the country for our retirement years). He would always take on the role of first driver of the day while I rode shotgun. As he traversed the side streets that led to the freeway entrance, I would fish out of my travel bag the CD that kicked off every single trip we ever took together: Willie Nelson's Greatest Hits. The twangy guitar and catchy chorus of "On the Road Again" soon filled the vehicle as my husband sipped his coffee and smiled from ear to ear.

"Off on another adventure with you, listening to Willie. Life can't get much better than this, babe," he would say with a smile.

If my husband had an alter-ego, it was Willie Nelson. In real life my husband was a clean-cut, suburban-dwelling, soccer-coaching family man who worked in an office all day, but when he listened to

Willie Nelson, he was an enigmatic drifter in the southwest, nursing a whiskey in a smoke-filled bar, refusing to let himself get tied down to any one woman for too long. Although my own musical taste leaned more towards Bon Jovi than Willie Nelson, I always joined in when my husband sang along with his favorite crooner.

When my husband died, Willie Nelson and "On the Road Again" disappeared from my life. I could not bear to hear that song again.

In fact, for a long time I drove in silence. Silence and tears. Until one day I decided I wanted the music back. Not Willie Nelson. Not my husband's song. My own song—a tune that would send me down the highway with the same sense of adventure and purposeful meandering as "On the Road Again."

My song turned out to be—surprisingly to me, a rock aficionado—another country song, which would have pleased my husband, I'm sure.

"Airstream Song." Track number six on Miranda Lambert's best-selling album, Revolution.

Like Willie Nelson, she sang about a life lived on the road, as a "gypsy," not tied to anything or anyone, traveling through town after town, breaking hearts along the way.

Except for the part about breaking hearts, which I am decidedly too old and uninclined to do, the song suits me perfectly. If I had my druthers, I would hit the road for good in an Airstream trailer.

So now my road trips begin with my own song. If my husband had once found his alter-ego in the rough-

hewn mystique of Willie Nelson, I have now discovered mine in young, sassy Miranda Lambert. Driving down the road with "Crazy Ex-Girlfriend" or "Mama's Broken Heart" blaring in the car, I am not a sad, middle-aged widow.

I am a take-no-prisoners, tough-talking, uber-confident twenty-something, tossing back my long, blonde hair, batting my overly black-mascaraed lashes, cursing the "dry towns" I speed through, and letting men know I won't hesitate to grab my shotgun or a can of kerosene if they mess with me.

One day the song I play when I toss my suitcase in the car and hit the road may change to one that doesn't center around a life lived on the move, without any ties.

But for now, this is my song.

The one about the life I want now.

The one that death can't take away from me.

DUTY OF CARE
(An essay written in Year Three)

Many years ago a situation arose related to work that resulted in my consulting an attorney. I was not interested in taking legal action against the individual in question. I just wanted to ensure that the situation did not continue, and Human Resources was not an option in this case.

The first issue the attorney wanted to determine was: Did my employer have a "duty of care" to protect me from the individual who was harassing me?

"Duty of care" is a legal term that basically means the employer is obligated to take all reasonable steps necessary to ensure the health, safety, and well-being of its employees; otherwise, the employer might be considered to be negligent.

If no "duty of care" exists, no obligation exists.

Like my employer's legal duty, my husband had a moral "duty of care" towards me during our marriage. He certainly did his best to ensure my health, safety, and well-being.

One of the things I had to learn as a widow, however, was that I needed to let go of the idea that any other human being had a "duty of care" towards me.

If I had biological children, I would have felt they had a duty of care towards me, but I do not. I have stepchildren, which is a different type of relationship. We love each other, but they live in another state, they are busy with their own lives, and they have a biological mother whose needs take precedence over mine. That's just the way it is. They do their best.

Obviously, parents have a duty of care towards their children, but my father is dead and my mother has Alzheimer's.

If a widow does have people around her who feel an ongoing duty of care towards her, she is indeed fortunate. Many do not have this type of support.

My three years of widowhood, coupled with conversations with many other widows, has led me to believe that the crux of the hurt feelings that we often (far too often) experience is the mistaken belief that a "duty of care" exists. How could the people who supposedly care about me forget my birthday or leave me alone on a holiday? Why haven't my old friends called lately? Why wasn't I invited to that gathering that was posted on Facebook? The list of painful incidents goes on and on, all due, in my opinion, to expectations that need to be adjusted. If expectations are not adjusted, hurt feelings will continue ad infinitum.

Realizing that the Creator is the only being who owes me a duty of care has been a freeing and even empowering experience. It has made it possible for me to detach in a healthy way from the actions of others and take responsibility for my own happiness. Detaching for me means realizing that just because I am not at the top of the list of priorities for the people in my life, it does not mean they do not care, and I can accept what they have to offer without expecting more. Taking responsibility for my own happiness means making the effort (and it is an effort) to make new friends, to make my own plans, to become as self-sufficient as possible, and to take the steps necessary to ensure I can forge ahead in this new life.

*And along the way, I continue to hear the voice of the one who **did** have a "duty of care" towards me, and he is saying "Atta Girl!"*

GREAT EXPECTATIONS

As I traveled around Grief Country in the early years of widowhood, I continually found myself returning to the State of Expectations.

I would often encounter fellow widows there, relating their own tales of shock and disappointment. They could not believe so many of the people in their lives had turned away from them or otherwise failed them in their time of need.

"I found out I had a lot of invisible friends," one of my widowed friends remarked wryly.

In one of my more cynical moments, I told a friend that the old chestnut, *"Let me know if there's anything I can do"* (sometimes said before disappearing from the scene) was code for *"Let me know when you're over it."*

What had I and my widowed friends expected from people? Was it realistic?

There are so many emotions involved when those we expect to support us do not do so—hurt feelings, disappointment, and anger, to name a few.

Hoping to avoid spiraling into resentment, I tried to take the emotion away and assess who had a "duty of care" to me, and who didn't.

Then I had to set about adjusting my expectations.

In the State of Expectations, I had traveled to and from cities like Why-Aren't-You-Calling-Me to I-Know-I-Would-Have-Been-Invited-If-He-Were-Still-Alive to What-About-All-The-Times-I-Was-There-For-You.

I tried to stop visiting those towns and began spending more time in the village of Lowered Expectations. Occasionally, I found myself in the restful territory of Unexpected Support, bolstered by the care of people I did not anticipate would play an important part in my journey through widowhood.

The fact that not everyone grieves in the same manner complicates the issue of expectations. One widow may depend for months on a nightly phone call from a friend or a relative; another widow might find such attention stifling or smothering. One may want "space"; another may not. A widow may not even know what she needs from others until the death occurs. Then she has to find a way to communicate these expectations to people who may or may not be willing or able to do what is requested.

It can be exhausting and frustrating. Why can't they *just know*? Dealing with the shock of widowhood is hard enough. Then a widow has to try to make it easier for everyone else?

And how exactly does a widow do that? We don't want to make others feel obligated and we know that when people don't want to do something, they often don't say "no"; they just quietly slip away or plead other commitments. By voicing our needs, we may risk losing them altogether.

This happened to me, and it has happened to other widows I know.

I recalled my days as a full-time caregiver for my husband, and how shortly before his death I came across articles on the internet addressing caregiver needs. Set up a web page, one person advised, and list all the items you need help with—meals, yard work, etc.—while you are caring for your loved one. People can sign up or let you know how they can help.

What would a widow's "needs" list look like? I wondered, and eventually realized it would be similar in many ways to the needs list of a caregiver.

What a Widow May Need During First Three Months of Bereavement

- Help with funeral arrangements, memorial service, celebration of life, or other form of remembrance.

- Assistance with paperwork and phone calls. (There are a myriad of agencies, institutions, and businesses that need to be notified of a death.)

- Transportation for children.

- Homework assistance for children.

- Offers to babysit children so the widow can attend a grief support group, occasional social activity, or church/faith services.

- Grocery shopping. (People have no idea how easily this simple task can trigger grief. I had to bypass the aisles with my husband's favorite foods for months.)

- Volunteers to perform the type of work that her husband might have done inside and outside the house, or a list of vendors who can handle these tasks (with prices).

- Emotional support via: phone calls, texts, letters, or in-person visits.

- Occasional follow-up cards letting the widow know you care about her, beginning weeks after the "sorry for your loss" cards have been put away. (She was probably still in the State of Numbness when those cards arrived.)

- A letter not about her late husband but about HER, letting her know all the things you are grateful for in your relationship. (Many widows would appreciate this bolstering of their self-esteem.)

- Someone to sit and listen for an hour as she talks about her husband, her life, or whatever is on her mind.

It's a lot, isn't it? And this list is by no means complete. How many friends or relatives are willing to do these things for a widow? How hard must it be for her to ask? Ideally, I wish every widow had a "widow advocate" who would distribute such a list to the widow's friends and relatives and say, *If you're willing to do any of these things, put a checkmark, write your name at the top, and give it back to me.* That would spare the widow from being in the difficult position of asking for help herself.

A widowed friend shared her opinion of the most important thing someone can and should do for a widow: "Acknowledge her loss."

It can be hurtful and jarring to attend a function attended by people one hasn't seen since the death of one's husband and listen to them say, "Nice to see you" or some other generic greeting without acknowledging the loss. I recall encountering one relative at a reception who appeared to go to some effort to specifically avoid acknowledging my loss. "Oh, hi," he said. "We haven't seen you … (pausing for an awkward moment) … in a long time."

I expected him to say, "I'm sorry about Ron," and I was shocked when he didn't. Perhaps his expectation was that I might be upset if he mentioned my husband's name.

When the loss of a husband isn't acknowledged, it can leave a widow feeling as if his death really didn't matter that much, and that her ongoing suffering doesn't matter. Most widows aren't going to go into depth about their pain at a social function. A brief sentence or a hug can bring much comfort.

There will be other, more appropriate times when a widow might long to share her pain, but the great expectation of being heard is often short-lived.

Some people will listen with a desire to understand, but a widow quickly discovers that most people are just not that interested in immersing themselves in the sorrowful waters of widowhood. They may have many valid reasons—perhaps it triggers memories of their own losses, it depresses them, or it conflicts with their ideas about whether it's healthy for the widow to keep talking about her loss—but in my opinion, there is another reason many people do not want to hear about what it's like to be a widow.

C'mon, it can't be THAT bad, can it?

They simply cannot believe widowhood is as bad as it is. The depth of the pain and the profound impact it has on virtually every aspect of a widow's life are impossible to convey, and if a widow continues to try to enlighten individuals who have this attitude, she will only grow more frustrated and resentful.

Over the course of my life, I've had reasons to be resentful. I saw at an early age, however, what resentment does to people, and I decided I did not want to be like those individuals. Like starving coyotes, resentment and bitterness will pounce upon and devour any chance of a happy, meaningful life. Just as I had done as a child in a dysfunctional home, as a widow I had to figure out a way to avoid resentment towards those who did not acknowledge either my loss or my ongoing grief.

The answer for me was to reframe the situation, and I used the dual process model proposed by psychologists Stroebe and Shut to do so.

In their paper, "The Dual Process Model of Coping with Bereavement," they presented a model of oscillation between loss-oriented activities and restoration-oriented activities. Earlier in this book I mentioned that I had followed this model instinctively after entering "normal" grief.

They also recommended "taking time off" from grief.

I decided to reframe all those occasions when people were ignoring my grief, instead choosing to view them as providing my "time off" from grief.

Reframing meant these individuals were not insensitive and uncaring. No, they were now de facto facilitators for my "time off" sessions, my tour guides for brief sojourns back to the land outside Grief Country. They were providing me a space where grief didn't exist. They were offering me laughter and conversation and a break from remembering the love of my life and the magnitude of what I had lost.

Was I just "giving them a pass"? I don't think so. I could not control whether or not anyone behaved towards me the way they "should." If I allowed myself to be resentful, it was only going to hurt me, not them. Reframing the situation in conjunction with a professionally constructed grief theory made me feel as if I was making a logical, rational, and mentally healthy choice.

Adjusting my expectations and reframing the responses of those around me was liberating.

The need for validation and acknowledgment had to be addressed through other means, however, so after I spent some time in the village of Lowered Expectations, I traveled to the vast region of Grief Country called Outside Support. It is often the next stop for those to whom no one owes a "duty of care."

In the chapter called "The Wild West," I discuss outside support in greater detail. Without the help of many kindly strangers, frankly, I don't know what I would have done.

A final note about expectations—one which to me is the most important issue. *What are my expectations for my life now?* was a question I asked myself time and time again.

Years ago I was an avid fan of figure skating. I attended every ice skating show that came to town, and I recorded my favorites (Scott Hamilton, Katarina Witt, Kristi Yamaguchi, Michelle Kwan, Paul Wylie) on VHS tapes so I could watch them more than once.

When the shocking news came that young Ekaterina Gordeeva's husband and pairs figure skating partner, Sergei Grinkov, had died from a sudden heart attack, I was struck by something she said about her loss. "I feel... *disappointed* in life," she said. Disappointed? At the time I wondered if her imperfect grasp of English had caused her to use the wrong word.

After I became a widow, I realized she had it exactly right. After the unbearable pain subsided, even after the initial readjustment and reengagement in life took place, a heavy layer of disappointment covered me. The horrifying thought, *Oh my God, how did this become my life?* was replaced by a more resigned realization: Oh. So this is now my life.

I had to find a way to adjust my expectations of my life going forward so that I would not sink into the shallow pockets of quicksand that are commonly found in Grief Country's State of Disappointment—pockets not deep enough to completely disappear into, but deep enough to prevent any movement. Pockets of quicksand that can keep a widow "stuck."

What do I expect from my life now? I don't expect to be happy to the extent that I was happy with my husband, but I do expect ever-increasing moments of joy and laughter. My former (pre-widowhood) expectation of "happiness" has been replaced by an expectation of peace and contentment. I expect my current relationships to continue and I expect to develop many more new friendships. I expect that more bad things will happen to me, and I expect that I will be able to handle them. I expect that some amazing, unexpectedly wonderful things will happen to me, and I expect I will be astonished, given the amount of time I spend in the village of Lowered Expectations!

Adjusting expectations may be one of the biggest challenges a widow faces. Every widow has to adjust her expectations of her new life, decide what her expectations are of her friends and family, and decide how she will handle it if those expectations are not met.

I almost entitled the next chapter, "Great Expectations: Part 2," as it focuses on a related topic: what happens when simply lowering or adjusting expectations isn't enough to sustain a relationship.

LETTING GO

In the early days of grief studies, the experts said one must "let go" of the spouse who has passed away.

In more recent years this thinking has changed. Now grievers are encouraged to maintain continuing bonds with their loved one, if desired, in whatever manner is helpful to them. Having conversations with them, keeping their photos displayed in the home, etc., are now viewed as perfectly healthy ways of dealing with their loss. Unless the attachment is pathological, "letting go" is not something widows necessarily need to do, the grief experts have concluded.

But while widows may not need to sever bonds with their departed husbands, "letting go" often occurs anyway as other relationships suddenly end.

Like friendships, for example. I've met very few widows whose friendships remained unchanged after the deaths of their husbands. The widows I know who kept their same circle of friends are all older widows (over 65). Two of my elderly relatives by marriage were widowed within a few years of each other, and their friends were women whom they had known for many years—some for their entire lives, as they lived in the same town where they had grown up. A good many were also widowed.

That is not to say that widows over 65 don't lose friendships, only that I've observed that among younger widows there seems to be a lot of "letting go" that takes place. It's often unexpected and hurtful, as friends pull away for many reasons. A widow's sadness can be too depressing. A married friend may feel as if she can now no longer discuss her own life and problems because they might be seen as too trivial. A friend who is still part of a couple may find it awkward to include the widow as a "single," so the invitations gradually disappear. Friends sometimes decide that "she really should be moving on by now" (whatever that means) and the widow's failure to meet that friend's arbitrary timeline becomes grounds for dropping her.

There are just as many reasons a widow might be the one to pull away. Her friend doesn't understand the depth of her pain or the vast extent to which her life has suddenly changed. Her friend may have made hurtful or careless comments that cannot be set aside. Her friend may have mistakenly decided that "tough love" and exhortation are what the widow needs at a time when those are the *last* things she needs.

"They just don't get it." I have heard widows express that sentiment many, many times. We want our friends to understand what we are going through without actually experiencing the death of their own husbands. Yes, it's illogical but true.

When my husband had brain cancer, I felt as if there was a "veil" between us. The cognitive changes caused by the tumor in his frontal lobe were subtle but caused great anguish for me. I could not understand what he was going through, and he could not understand what I was going through. We were no longer on the same side of the veil, and we never would be again. Accepting that fact was difficult but necessary.

I was trying to explain certain aspects of widowhood to a married cousin when I suddenly had a vision of the same veil between us. It was so vivid, I felt as if I could actually touch it. In that moment I accepted the fact that I could not pierce the veil with my words. I could only try to express the experience of widowhood in a way that might open her eyes to see me a bit more clearly through the veil.

I realized the anger that widows express towards their friends who don't "get it" is misdirected. We are not really mad at our friends. Our frustration and anger should really be directed at "the veil." It is the veil that we should hate, the veil that it has caused this separation and, too often, this sacrifice of relationships.

When my husband was sick, sometimes I wanted to cry out to him—illogically, because it wasn't his fault—*Why did you have to go and change on me?* But in this case, as widows, we are the ones who have changed. Perhaps our friends want to cry out to us, *Why did you have to go and change on me?*

Like marriage, motherhood, and divorce, widowhood can precipitate a major shakeup in female relationships.

Many widows find solace in the company of other widows, but my experience has made me cautious about investing too much, too soon in these relationships.

I met Jenny at a caregiver support group. My husband had died nine months earlier, but I was still taking care of my mother. Jenny's husband had a life-limiting illness, and she was his full-time caregiver. We clicked right away.

A few months later Jenny's husband died. Devastated, she emailed me. "How did you ever survive this?" she asked. She fell into a deep depression and I did my best to encourage her not to give up. For about a year we exchanged heartfelt weekly emails and met occasionally for lunch. Finally Jenny started to become reengaged in life, traveling to visit family and returning to part-time work. The friends who "just didn't understand" in the beginning were once again embraced. In one email she mentioned becoming friendly with a neighbor who had lost his wife. Lunch plans were made, but she cancelled twice. Then the emails stopped.

She didn't need me anymore.

It was a briefly hurtful experience, but I learned a valuable lesson. Like the care teams that surrounded my husband, widows can surround other widows with compassion and understanding in a highly charged emotional environment, but that doesn't necessarily translate into lasting friendships. The shared experience of widowhood may eventually fade over time due to a lack of common interests, conflicting world views, or other differences. Jenny and I really didn't have much in common other than our bereavement. I never regretted the time I spent trying to help her through her depression. I only wish I hadn't assumed that it meant we would be long-term friends.

On the other hand, many widow friendships strengthen over time. I cherish the friendships I have developed with a few of the many widows I have met since my husband died—even the ladies I "met" online.

Sometimes letting go of the friendships that predated widowhood can be temporary, as was the case with my friend Jenny and her old friends who "didn't get it" once she became a widow. There was a brief time when I, too, let go of a friendship only to return to that person eventually. However, I was a bit wiser by that time and realized that although our relationship could be restored, it would not necessarily be the same as it was before.

Another type of "letting go" that some of my widowed friends have commonly experienced is the relationship with their late husband's family. I have heard many stories from widows who have been deeply hurt by being "dropped"—some gradually, and some abruptly.

My husband's parents died before we married, but I always had a friendly relationship with his siblings. They all got along famously, but they were increasingly busy with their individual families so my husband and I saw them infrequently. Following my husband's brain cancer diagnosis, the communication and visits increased, as might be expected. After he died, though, my contact with them dwindled as things went back to the way they had been before—an occasional email or visit. Distance and other factors contributed to what felt to me like another loss, but I'm grateful for the still-cordial connection that remains. (I discuss my relationship with my husband's adult children in the chapter entitled, "Step-Widowhood.")

Attending events with a late husband's family can also bring into sharp relief the issues a widow might face related to a loss of identity and status, as well as a realization that it may be time to "let go."

"So are you related to the bride?" I wasn't sure how to answer that question, which was broached by one of the young bride's new in-laws at a reception held several weeks after their destination wedding. In the past I would most likely have been standing next to my husband, who would have said, "I'm the bride's great-uncle" and then introduced me as his wife. Now, however, I stood alone.

"Um, well, her grandmother was my husband's sister," I replied, stumbling a bit over "was" versus "is"—not wanting to explain that my husband was dead. "So I guess I'm related by marriage," I finished.

But was I? The marriage didn't technically exist anymore, so what exactly was my status in this situation?

I was just a guest. It was actually gracious of the bride to invite me at all, since she hardly knew me. I had an enjoyable time visiting with my husband's large extended family, but additional invitations (excluding those from his siblings) were not forthcoming. My husband had been our connection, and that connection no longer existed.

As someone who is not particularly fond of big gatherings, it didn't bother me too much, but I have spoken with a number of widows who have been immensely hurt by what they perceived as another loss. If they remain "social media friends" with their husband's relatives, for example, they may learn of their omission from his family's events by suddenly being confronted with photos from the festive occasion.

It can get so complicated. If the husband's family has continued to invite the widow (and her children) to family gatherings after the death of their son, what happens if she starts dating again? How will they feel about including a guy who might be seen as a "replacement" for their son?

Grief is triggered by different things for different people. Sometimes, through no fault of our own, our very presence in the lives of our husband's family members can serve as a trigger for their grief.

It's incredibly difficult for a widow to navigate her way through Grief Country's State of Letting Go. Many of us are abruptly faced with the fact that the relationships we have taken for granted, possibly for decades, are far more fragile than we realized.

Letting go can be painful, but the effort expended in maintaining relationships that no longer serve us as widows can be better spent in developing new relationships that will enrich our lives—sometimes to a degree that amazes us.

"I realized one day that every single friend I had before my husband's death was no longer in my life." The widow who told me this lost her husband ten years earlier. "Of course it was hurtful when they all disappeared, but I have been blessed with so many new relationships that I never expected—truly deep friendships that I am so grateful for and that I'm confident will last."

If she hadn't escaped from Grief Country's State of Fear—where some widows cling to failing relationships because they don't want to find themselves dwelling even temporarily in the State of Loneliness—she would not have the abundant life she enjoys today. She didn't let go of her husband—the love, the memories, and even a feeling of connection remains—but she did let go of those with whom there was no longer a real relationship.

Letting go of relationships, letting go of yesterday's plans, letting go of what "used to be" and "was supposed to have been"... It is undeniably an excruciatingly painful process and one that takes every widow a different amount of time. No one has the right to rush any widow through it. What we *can* do when she lets something go is to take that empty hand, give it a squeeze, and say, "I'm still here for you."

CREDENTIALS
(An essay written in Year Two)

Many years ago I had a friend who was brilliant. She read voraciously and, unlike me, she retained nearly one hundred percent of what she learned. She spoke knowledgeably about everything from astrophysics to DNA sequencing. I usually didn't have the slightest idea what she was talking about.

"Unless the author of a book has credentials, either a number of professional designations or a doctorate, I don't bother reading it," she told me.

At the time I couldn't imagine having such specific requirements for those who could pass along their knowledge to me.

Now, however, I do.

Whenever I hear someone holding forth about life's great challenges and dispensing advice, whether it's across a dining room table, in church, on television talk shows, or in an auditorium, I silently ask the speaker one question.

What have you lost?

Of course, many people have suffered losses of which they never speak, so I often have no way of knowing the answer to that question. But there are times when it can be known, and I've been struck by the realization that the person speaking has not experienced great loss in their life—at least not loss as I now define it.

Am I too judgmental? Quite possibly. Nevertheless, the person I want to listen to is someone who has experienced the kind of loss that brings profound understanding, someone who is truly qualified to counsel others.

I don't require the authors of books I read to have any particular professional credentials. And I always try to take away whatever knowledge I can when listening to friends, counselors, pastors, or others.

But when it comes to true, deep wisdom and insight, for me the speaker's credibility always rests upon that one question: ***What have you lost?***

THE WILD WEST

As I spent more and more time in Grief Country, I began to reexamine the concept of "credentials" and the essay I wrote during Year Two.

I still regarded with skepticism most pontificating from folks who hadn't experienced great loss in their lives. However, I came to appreciate that when it comes to seeking help with grief, credentials can indeed matter.

"It's like the Wild West out there," a psychologist affiliated with one nonprofit organization told me. He was referring to the proliferation of individuals he believed had insufficient training to be guiding bereaved individuals through one of the most wrenching experiences of their lives.

I occasionally attended a widows' support group offered by his organization, and I was struck by how respectfully the facilitator listened to those in attendance before deftly steering the discussion toward greater understanding of the grief process.

All the support group counselors had degrees in psychology or social work, coupled with extensive backgrounds in grief counseling. There were firm guidelines in place to ensure the groups ran smoothly. Attendees were asked to "own their words," meaning that their comments should be about their own experiences rather than giving unsolicited advice or telling others what their experience of grief is, should be, or will be. The efficient functioning of the group as a whole was the priority, so a single individual was not allowed to dominate the discussion. Comparing losses was not permitted.

All grief support groups and grief counselors are not created equally.

The meetings I attended after my husband died were located in a hospital, a hospice, a church, a community center, and a nonprofit organization devoted solely to grief support. Some groups were facilitated by social workers, psychologists, and counselors, while others were led by widows without specific education or training in the field of grief.

I believe I benefited in some way from most of the meetings I attended, because even if I didn't receive any insight into my own grief on a particular day, it was rewarding to be able to support other bereaved individuals who needed someone to hear their story.

I appreciated the tiny, church-based group of widows who helped me strengthen the faith that had been shaken so badly. I was not a member of their congregation and I did not share some of their beliefs, but that made no difference. They welcomed me with open arms. Their meetings were "platitude-free" and surprisingly candid, led by a wonderful woman who had no formal training in grief yet possessed a wisdom that was born out of her own difficulties following widowhood.

Those "uncredentialed" widows helped me to find peace.

Another group I attended on two occasions was also peer-led, but I did not find it helpful, especially as one widow was allowed to dominate virtually the entire second meeting. The facilitator provided a few handouts that appeared to be somewhat outdated, referring to "stages" of grief, but otherwise she said very little. I came away from the two sessions I attended more depressed than when I arrived.

A support group for widows who had lost their husbands to glioblastoma multiforme was helpful because it focused on our shared experience of dealing with the aftermath of battling a rare disease that presents specific, unique challenges for a spouse.

My attendance at various support groups was spread over three years and was somewhat sporadic. As I entered my third year of widowhood, a sudden onslaught of difficulties in my life over a two-month period prompted me to seek individual counseling.

I found my counselor "accidentally" (as explained in the chapter entitled "A Show of Hands"), so I was extremely fortunate in that she was highly credentialed, with more than twenty-five years of experience as a grief counselor. In addition, she had experienced widowhood, which gave depth to her knowledge.

By the time I began to see my counselor, I had read a number of books about grief; however, it didn't occur to me to ask her if she subscribed to the "stage" or "phase" theories or another model of grief. It wasn't apparent from our sessions that she had a preference, so again, I was fortunate. Knowing what I know now, if I were ever to seek grief counseling again, I would ask the counselor about his or her thoughts about models of grief, and I would stay away from a counselor who still subscribed to theories centered around stages of grief.

A short time later I had the conversation with the psychologist who was concerned the grief counseling landscape had become a kind of "Wild West."

I inferred from his remarks that some of his concerns stemmed from the burgeoning number of for-profit entities offering training in grief that may range from weeks to months. Graduates of these programs earn a certificate that indicates they completed the prescribed courses, which are based upon the founder's beliefs about the grief process. Often those who obtain such a certificate have suffered their own losses and are seeking a way to help others. The students' goals may be to provide counseling services, lead support groups as a volunteer, or help the bereaved in other ways that don't require professional qualifications.

Conversely, there are also national associations that offer certification in thanatology ("certification" rather than a "certificate"). These associations require a bachelor's degree in a related discipline such as social services, psychology, or counseling, perhaps a master's degree, and many hours of hands-on experience in the field to be admitted to their programs.

To summarize, when a counselor says they are "certified in grief," some clarification and due diligence may be needed. A griever should ask someone with a certificate in grief studies the same questions about education, qualifications, counseling methods and goals, etc., that they would ask of a state-licensed counselor.

State-licensed grief counselors are not credentialed to diagnose or treat mental disorders or to conduct psychotherapy. They cannot prescribe medication and are required to refer clients to a medical professional if warranted. They can only counsel, listen, support, and coach those who are grieving. Grief counselors are required to inform new clients about what they can and cannot do prior to beginning any counseling, as well as provide their state licensing information.

One reason "credentials" can matter is that giving the wrong advice to a widow who might be suffering from major depressive disorder or prolonged grief disorder, for example, can be extremely detrimental. She needs a trained professional to make the appropriate diagnosis and recommend appropriate treatment.

Also, individuals who have not kept pace with new developments in the field of grief studies might be promoting theories that have long since been discredited. Promulgating these theories might leave a widow feeling frustrated that she's not grieving "in the right way" (for example, not going through the discredited "five stages of grief").

Even though I believe I was helped by both credentialed and uncredentialed individuals, I can understand the concerns expressed by my acquaintance.

Many widows receive all the support they need from family and friends. Other widows may find what they need through widows' social groups, which might include limited grief support. I attended a few meetings of one such group in my third year of widowhood and met some wonderful, caring ladies. Although my own needs by that time were strictly social and not grief support, I was always struck by the palpable relief on the faces of new widows in attendance as they told their stories and received support from the other widows.

***

The Wild West is a region of Grief Country that requires caution. It includes not only support groups and counselors—licensed and unlicensed—but all the other advice for widows "out there." It can be challenging to sift through the overwhelming amount of information contained in books, newspaper and magazine articles, blog posts, television and radio programs, news segments, TED Talks, YouTube videos, and podcasts. Not to mention all those one-sentence quotations about grief that can appear on one's Facebook news feed.

When I became a widow, what I needed was not someone pushing me towards the light at the end of the tunnel; rather, I needed someone willing to stand next to me in the darkness, holding my hand as my eyes adjusted.

The individuals I met in grief support groups were my hand-holders, the ones who raised candles to illuminate the way forward but sensitively refrained from insisting that I sprint towards the light. They did not pressure me to be grateful or tell me that I must choose to be positive at a time when those words were meaningless to me. They let me be angry, negative, and completely devastated until I no longer needed to be any of those things.

Only then could thankfulness whisper in my ear. Only then could I begin to take baby steps away from the horror, the pain, the magnitude of what I had lost, and tentatively glance backwards with gratitude.

I am forever indebted to the bereaved strangers who circled wagons of empathy around me for so many months, and to the quiet, unobtrusive facilitators who knew when to speak and when to remain silent.

AFTERSHOCKS
(An essay written in Year Three)

I was born in earthquake country. When I was a toddler, my parents sold their starter home, which was situated atop a major fault line, and left the state of California. So I did not grow up, as I might otherwise have done, waiting for "The Big One" to hit.

As it turned out, I didn't escape "The Big One" after all.

When my husband was diagnosed with grade four brain cancer, our world began its violent shaking. If there had been slow warning rumblings beneath the surface of the ground we so confidently stood on, we hadn't felt them. No, the sudden upheaval of all that we had built so carefully took us by surprise, and it seemed as if I barely had time to grab my husband's hand before the pillars of our past, present, and future collapsed all around us. When the ground stopped moving, I found myself alone in the rubble.

I still can hardly believe how fast it happened. So much destruction in so short a time.

Since emerging from the ruins, I've slowly begun erecting a new structure in which to dwell. Sometimes I've felt the aftershocks coming, feeling the slow buildup of white-hot emotion, the crashing to the ground of what might have been, the reality of having nothing to hold on to within my grasp as the walls started shaking. I've had time to run, to find terra firma in the comfort of my friends, my stepchildren, my widows' support group, my faith.

Other times the aftershocks have come suddenly, without warning, ranking high enough on the Richter Scale of widowhood that they have brought much of my house down around my feet again. I've angrily tossed aside the broken bricks, grabbed a trowel, and furiously thrown myself into reconstructing the walls of my new life with the gusto of an Amish farmer attempting to raise a barn in a day.

Twice, the aftershocks have been so strong that when cracks appeared beneath my feet and the earth began to open up, I closed my eyes, lifted my arms up in surrender, and allowed myself to fall forward. Both times, an unseen hand pulled me back from the edge of the abyss.

After an earthquake, the crust around the displaced fault plane must adjust, and it is this adjustment that creates an aftershock.

Aftershocks are a necessary evil. As I continue to adjust to this new landscape, I can expect aftershocks, and I cannot predict when they will strike. I have faith that one day the aftershocks will weaken to the point where I might even feel as if I am standing on stable ground once more.

I will keep building my house.

A SHOW OF HANDS

My two tiny dogs jockeyed for position in my lap as I sat in my oversized recliner. I scratched one of them behind the ears absent-mindedly as I stared out the window. My eyes were open but I was blind to the outside world, conscious of the presence of the gigantic fir trees across the street but unable to truly see them. I closed my eyes and, for the second time in the twenty-seven months since my husband's death, I thought about taking my own life.

The pain had been building inside for several months. A series of events had occurred that had plunged me into deep depression.

I sat in my chair, eyes shut, willing the troubling thoughts away. My mind was blank for a long while, I'm not even sure how long, but eventually thoughts began to form . . . *Just breathe. . . Remember the last time. . .*

I recalled my previous battle with hopelessness, six months after my husband's death, when I had been overwhelmed by the exhaustion and stress caused by 24-hour caregiving for a mother with Alzheimer's disease and mental illness. At that time I had held in my hand the pills that I believed would provide an escape from my pain, but instead I had opted to reach out to strangers for help, and the sinister darkness had lifted.

Let it pass, let it pass. . . Within an hour the dark thoughts were gone, and as I gazed out the window, I imagined them floating away on the breeze that gently shook the tall fir trees across the street.

I knew what I had to do. As before, I needed to reach out for help. Ironically, a few weeks earlier I had prepared a resource list for widows in conjunction with a fundraiser I had volunteered for. I called one of the grief counselors on the list and made an appointment, crying periodically as I tried to explain to the kind woman on the phone why I needed help.

Shortly afterwards, I flipped on the television set and was surprised to see the *"Breaking News"* chyron at the bottom of the screen.

Robin Williams, the famous comedian and actor, had committed suicide.

Shock and sadness washed over me, just like it did with everyone else across the country. I had no idea why he had chosen to take his own life. It seemed from early reports that even his friends and family were unaware of the extent of his suffering.

That evening I received a text from a relative. *"Did you hear about Robin Williams committing suicide today? Such terrible news."*

I stared at the text and decided not to reply. What could I say? *Yeah, I heard. BTW, I thought about killing myself this morning.*

I was so disconnected from everyone at that point that no one had a clue as to how seriously depressed I was. And I couldn't tell them.

More than a year later, I told that relative my story. Naturally, she was shocked. "You should have called…" Maybe I should have, but I didn't think she would understand. And at that point, what I needed was professional help, which, thankfully, I got.

I resolved to do everything possible to avoid going down that dark path ever again.

In an earlier chapter, I wrote about trying to make my way across the "monkey bars" as I tried to rebuild my life. One of the monkey bars I grabbed was professional grief counseling. Another was a visit to my doctor to discuss my depression. The "monkey bar" of accepting the fact that for a few months I needed to be on low-dose anti-depressants was a particularly hard swing for me. I was someone who usually "toughed it out," but this time, it was obvious, that strategy was not going to work.

There were two more "monkey bars" that hung between me and optimal mental health: anger and determination.

As self-destructive thoughts grew farther and farther away, a healthy, motivating anger kicked in. I was NOT going to fall into the abyss or let anyone else's hurtful actions push me over the edge. I was going to rise from the ashes. It was about this time that I wrote my essay, "Duty of Care."

I decided I was going to be okay.

My largely secret struggle with hopelessness, I came to learn, was not at all unique.

* * *

"How many of you in this room have had thoughts of suicide? A show of hands. . . ?" The woman who was conducting an informal discussion with a group of widows had posed this question.

I glanced around the room and noticed nearly every hand was raised. Almost every one of these pleasant, highly functioning, and outwardly calm women had considered ending her own life.

Of course, many widows don't even think about doing such a thing. Are widows who attend functions with other widows or grief support groups simply representative of a minority who lack social or family support, making them more vulnerable to dark thoughts? I don't know. There doesn't seem to be a lot of information "out there" about widows and suicide; however, according to psychologists Margaret and Wolfgang Stroebe, "... statistics have confirmed that the widowed are at particularly high risk of taking their own lives." They go on to state, "Highest risk occurs in the weeks and months closest to loss..."[1]

Is age a factor? More than half of widows are over age 65, as might be expected, given the different life spans of men and women. The National Alliance on Mental Illness reports that "Unmarried and widowed individuals as well as those who lack a supportive social network also have elevated rates of depression." They also point out that "Depression is the single most significant risk factor for suicide in the elderly population."[2]

Many widows lose their husbands after a prolonged period of caregiving, as I did. The deleterious effects of caregiving can continue into widowhood, according to the authors of "Bereavement After Caregiving,"

Richard Schulz, Randy Hebert, and Kathrin Boerner. "When the death does occur, the caregiver enters bereavement already compromised with high levels of depression and anxiety..." In their work with caregivers for loved ones with dementia, they discovered that "...30%... were at risk for clinical depression 1 year post-death..."[3]

I can only assume that their findings related to caregivers for loved ones with dementia could also apply to caregivers for loved ones with similar cognitive issues.

Whose responsibility is it to make sure a depressed widow gets professional help so she doesn't become a suicide statistic? Who has a "duty of care" towards her? What if friends or family are absent or do not feel such an obligation?

I hope that as a society, we can pay closer attention to the widows around us—of all ages—who need someone to assume a "duty of care" towards them before it's too late.

We don't need any more widows to stumble off the backroads of Grief Country and disappear altogether.

STEP-WIDOWHOOD

I have coined a term for myself: "step-widow." I am a widow who does not have biological children, but I do have stepchildren. I value the caring relationship we've been able to develop.

Not every step-widow is so fortunate.

I met Eve at a bereavement workshop shortly after our husbands' deaths. We discovered that we lived very close to each other, our husbands had the same first name, and both had served in the military. They had even been interred at the same veterans' cemetery within a few feet of each other.

Eve visited me at my home one afternoon, a few weeks after we met. I asked how she had been since our meeting at the workshop and was taken aback when she burst into tears.

"My stepchildren have been so awful to me," she told me. "I don't understand it. Their father got sick just a couple of years after we got married and I took care of him for the next eight years. I told my husband I didn't want his retirement money or anything. All I wanted him to leave me was the house because I need somewhere to live. Now his kids are demanding that I try to find their *mother's* will. She died, like, twenty years ago. I don't understand it. They're suddenly acting cold towards me. It feels like they're looking for a way to take everything away from me. Their dad would be furious."

"I'm so sorry," I said. "That's pretty low." Our visit ended with a promise to meet again, but soon afterwards she called and told me she had decided to move closer to her siblings. "I don't even want to be in this house anymore," she said. "I thought I would live here and my stepchildren would visit, but everything's changed now that their dad is gone."

June was an elderly woman who lived a few blocks away from me in the retirement community where my husband and I had moved after his diagnosis of brain cancer. As I was picking up my mail one day, she waved at me as she exited her car on the way to her own mailbox.

"I don't know if you heard," she said with tears in her eyes, "but my husband died last week."

I offered her a hug and my condolences. We chatted about her husband for a few minutes. Then she said, "I'm so shocked by the way my husband's kids have behaved. They told me it was important that I go right away to the Social Security office and the girls offered to take me. I thought that was nice of them, but when I returned home, I found out their brother had gone through the house and taken all the things they wanted. My husband kept a basket of coins next to the recliner on the floor, and he used to clean out his pockets and drop the change into the basket. There was probably a few hundred dollars' worth of change in there. His son even took that basket!"

"What? They shouldn't be taking anything unless it was left to them in your husband's will or had been promised to them," I said. "And it takes time to settle an estate."

"I know," she said, wiping her eyes. "He left everything to me but he didn't really have anything of value. We were living on Social Security and we struggled sometimes just to pay the space rent here." She paused. "The thing is, I would have given them stuff. Whatever they wanted. They didn't even wait. They just went behind my back. As if it hasn't been hard enough to lose my husband... I'm just so hurt!"

Hurt. That word kept coming up over and over again whenever I spoke with women I knew who were "step-widows."

Much has been written about the "secondary losses" of widowhood, but seldom is it mentioned that relationships with stepchildren are also often lost.

I met one young woman whose husband died suddenly, and her husband's ex-wife promptly informed her that she would no longer be allowed to visit the two very young children she had taken into her home on regular visits for three years, children she had bathed, dressed, comforted when they fell down, and tucked into bed at night with a lullaby.

Sometimes it's the step-widow who ends the relationship. I recalled a phone conversation I had with a woman whose husband was battling brain cancer. A social worker had given the woman my phone number so I could share the experience my husband and I had as we struggled with brain cancer.

"It's hard enough dealing with all the terrible changes my husband is going through," the woman told me over the phone. "But his teenage daughter is making everything worse." Her stepdaughter was in denial about her father's illness and expected him to do everything for her the way he used to. When he couldn't, she took it out on her stepmother. The already shaky relationship between the two of them was being further destroyed by the devastating effects of brain cancer. The situation was so stressful that the woman had already decided that if her husband died, she would have nothing more to do with her stepdaughter.

I listened as she vented all her frustrations about her stepdaughter. At one point I tried to suggest she not close the door entirely.

"Believe me," I said. "I understand. But if your husband passes away, she may need you." I explained how my stepchildren and I had created a better relationship during my husband's illness and how we had eventually helped each other deal with our grief.

"I don't know," she said skeptically. "I can't see that happening with us. At this point, I don't even want to try."

It was our one and only conversation. The social worker later told me the woman's husband had passed away, but I never knew how things turned out with her stepdaughter.

Sometimes the bond between a stepmother and her stepchildren is tenuous, yet endures.

"Bill had been estranged from his kids for years before I came along," my friend Linda said. "That didn't seem right to me, so a couple of years after we married, I found a way to send a message to his daughter on Facebook."

Linda and her stepdaughter met, and gradually, Linda's husband Bill became a part of his adult children's lives again. They had seven or eight years together before Bill's death.

It seemed to be an encouraging step-widow story, because Linda continued to maintain a relationship with her stepchildren. Since she didn't have biological children, she had a family that she would not otherwise have had. As time went on, however, the contact began to become more one-sided and gradually lessened. Linda eventually realized that she wasn't going to be an integral part of her stepchildren's lives. That realization was disappointing and somewhat hurtful, but Linda accepted the change gracefully. She moved out of the area, but she continued to stay in touch with her stepchildren.

In my five years of widowhood, I have heard more stories like Linda's than those of continuing bonds.

My stepchildren and I have had to work hard to maintain our bond. It hasn't always been easy. We have faced challenges of physical distance, uncertainty as to where we fit into each other's lives, occasional hurt feelings, and managing the delicate balance of the wants and needs of a biological mother, a stepmother, and adult stepchildren who are starting to raise their own families.

I don't take our relationship for granted, as I recognize that the promise we once made to their father—a promise to remain a family—may one day seem less important to keep as the years go by or life circumstances change. I remain hopeful, however, that it will stand the test of time.

So what are the factors that seem to affect whether or not a stepchild and stepmother remain in contact following the death of the father/husband?

I could find no research on this topic, so this is my own assessment of the primary issues:

- The stepmother's desire to continue the relationship.

- The stepchild's desire to continue the relationship.

- The length of the relationship prior to the death.

- The quality of the relationship.

- The age of the stepchild.

- The expectations of the stepchild after the death (i.e., inheritance, possessions, etc.).

- The attitude of the biological mother towards the stepmother (i.e., her willingness/ unwillingness to support a continued relationship).

- The impact of a stepmother's remarriage, if it occurs.

The first four factors are self-explanatory.

When it comes to the age of the stepchildren, the younger they are, the more likely it seems that both parties would wish to continue the relationship. However, that's where the attitude of the biological mother is the deciding factor. For a variety of reasons, she may decide to sever the relationship between the children and the step-widow.

What a heartbreaking situation for a step-widow to face. So many wives throw themselves into a "mothering" role when they marry a man with small children. They make an emotional investment and grow to love the kids, expecting they will be in her life for the foreseeable future.

If a biological mother ends the relationship, it is a secondary loss that is unique to a step-widow. A widow with biological children does not have to worry that someone else will make the decision as to whether she sees those children ever again.

The holiday season can be difficult for any widow, including those with biological children, whom they may or may not see at family celebrations. It's also a challenge for a step-widow like me. My stepchildren alternate spending Thanksgiving Day and Christmas Day with their biological mother or their in-laws. We try to see each other during the holiday season when we can, but I know that it's very unlikely I will ever see them on the actual holidays.

So many step-widows face the challenge of finding "a place to go" on those days. It can be especially disconcerting for the step-widow who is realizing her bond with her stepchildren is weakening. If they are adults, they may have made it a point to visit "Dad" on Christmas, but are they going to go to the same trouble to visit "Dad's wife?" And if they are minor children, the custody agreement that provided for splitting or sharing holidays between biological parents is immediately null and void when the father dies. How many ex-wives make sure their children see their stepmother on Thanksgiving or Christmas after an ex-husband's death? (If they do, there's a special place in heaven for them.)

The sudden changes related to holidays and stepchildren can be very demoralizing to a step-widow, especially in the first year when she's trying to figure out her new status among those she thought were her family members.

One year I was spending the holidays with my husband, confident in my status. The next few years I was bouncing around from place to place, trying to be a pleasant addition to Other People's Christmases. Once, due to the weather, I found myself alone on Christmas. It didn't feel great, but I shrugged it off. After all, I'd been through worse. (Perspective had crept back into my life by then.)

I always try to remember that there are others in a similar position—the divorced woman who has no family, the woman who has moved to a new city, the single woman whose only child has died, the woman whose children live far away or whose children tell her "It's the in-laws turn." As time goes on, the holidays are getting a little easier for me, but there's no denying it's a hard time for step-widows.

Then there is the issue of money and possessions. Every few years we read the headlines about a Hollywood celebrity who dies, often leaving behind a wife who is not the biological mother of his children. Within a few months stories begin to emerge of court battles between the step-widow and her stepchildren over the celebrity's estate.

Even though the "estate" in question may pale next to that of a Hollywood celebrity, I have met a number of step-widows who found themselves in disputes with adult stepchildren (and sometimes an ex-wife who is the mother of minor children).

Regardless of the particular circumstances of any one case, it is still a challenge that is unique to a step-widow's situation. Except in rare cases, biological children do not sue a biological mother over money and possessions.

Besides the holidays, there are other occasions where being a step-widow requires a large dose of humility. Whereas a biological mother will be central to a wedding ceremony of a child, for example, after a father's death the step-widow may be relegated to the role of "guest." She may not be seated with "parents" and she may not be included in photographs. She may or may not be invited to events which the father would have attended with her by his side, such as children's birthday parties or graduations, perhaps out of deference to the biological mother or perhaps because the bond is already beginning to weaken.

Will the step-widow accept whatever relationship is possible or will she decide it's too detrimental to her self-esteem and causes too much pain? I have spoken with a number of widows who have struggled with this question and opted to simply bow out of the relationship.

As much as our society tries to promote the idea that we can successfully "blend" families if we follow the guidelines of the experts, the truth is that stepfamilies are stitched together with a far weaker thread than biological families, and this thread can snap in an instant, via divorce or death.

Obviously, every step-widow is not a saint and there are stepchildren who complain about the treatment they received at the hands of their stepmothers. I can only say that my experience and my conversations have been with widows who were not, in my estimation, "evil stepmothers."

The unique challenges faced by step-widows underscore the diversity of widow experiences. Widows who aren't stepmothers will never set foot in the State of Step-Widowhood.

It can be a pleasant place to dwell, where the children of the beloved father and husband comfort his widow and vice versa, forming an even stronger bond. Or it can be an achingly lonely place, where a step-widow suffers the secondary loss of her husband's legacy on earth, the children who share his eyes, his laugh, and his name. Step-widowhood can either break your heart for a second time or help to heal it, transforming a stepmother and stepchildren into a singularly beautiful example of love and family.

With cities as diverse as You'll-Always-Be-A-Mom-To-Us and I-Was-Only-Being-Polite-For-Dad's-Sake, it can be a state of either joy or sorrow—unique in Grief Country.

DANCING
(An essay written in Year Three)

"**L**eft foot first, four steps forward, four steps back, turn and touch, and touch, then chassé to the left, and pivot and turn..."

The line dance instructor is wearing a wireless microphone, calling out the steps as he weaves effortlessly between the rows of students, deftly navigating his way past the misplaced foot here, the careless elbow there, allowing us to see how a proper Mexican salsa is done.

I am worn out after forty-five minutes of nonstop movement, but I gamely soldier on, ignoring the discomfort of my aging hips as I swing my chubby left leg forward and across to the right side of my body one more time.

I stumble a bit, and within seconds I am hopelessly lost, unable to catch up to my fellow neophyte line dancers. A wave of emotion sweeps over me, and I *freeze in place, a statue in the middle of a busy and crowded town square.*

"Some of you are thinking too much," *the instructor warns us sternly from his reclaimed position at the front of the class.* "Counting steps won't make you a dancer. Don't overthink it."

*I know his remarks are not necessarily directed solely at me, but I feel a protest rising to my lips, nevertheless. That's **not** what's happening with me, I want to say to him. You have no idea...*

*I am not counting the steps. I'm not overthinking; in fact, just the opposite. I'm over-**feeling**, as has happened time and time again during this class.*

My husband taught me how to dance. When we started dating, he couldn't believe I had managed to reach my thirties without ever having attempted to dance. He quickly realized that unlike him, I had no natural rhythm or grace. Painstakingly, he showed me how to move my feet, how to move my body to the music, and how to let him lead. "Just look at me and I'll take care of the rest," *he said, so I looked into his eyes instead of down at my feet and trusted that he knew what he was doing.*

I slowly gained confidence, and soon I mastered the waltz, the West Coast swing, the cha cha, and a few other dances. We danced in a beautifully restored, old-fashioned ballroom in the heart of the city, we danced in a Western bar that played the country music he loved, and we danced in a posh lounge on an Alaskan cruise ship.

We danced on a Saturday night in our dining room, right after we found out he had brain cancer, a few days before surgery, thinking it might be our last dance.

And we danced again a few weeks later, in the same dining room, after he regained his ability to walk.

"Okay, are we ready for the Bicycle Waltz? We learned that one last week—remember?" *The instructor walks back to the center of the assemblage of dancers and waits for the music to start. I will myself to pay attention as he calls out,* "Okay... step left forward..."

I fight back the tears that have suddenly welled up in my eyes. What am I doing here? It can never be the way it once was. I will never again feel his arm around my waist, confidently gliding me across the floor, his eyes sparkling with happiness.

We had cherished our slow dance when he came home from the hospital, but the merciless tumor in his brain had returned to rob him of his mobility, and eventually, his life.

"Turn half step left, then right step back!" *The instructor bellows as I instinctively turn left then step back with my right foot.* **Wait!** *Did I just do that automatically, a split second before he called out the steps?*

"Step left together!" *he shouts, and I realize I know the steps. I do them without thinking, and more importantly, without* **feeling**. *The sadness quick-steps its way out of my body as I give myself over to the* movement, the flow, the rhythm. Nothing else exists except the dance.

As we transition to the Cuban Shuffle, I stumble a little, but this time it's because I am indeed overthinking the steps. No matter. I was certain I would never dance again after I lost my patient, private dance instructor, the love of my life, but I am doing it.

My steps are uncertain at times and my turns are slower than everyone else's, but I am dancing.

I am dancing.

PART III

REFLECTING

EXPERTS (PART 1)

It was a sunny but cold spring day in 2005. I was sitting on a mattress on the floor of my friend Khadija's bedroom. She sat next to me, silent, as we watched Oprah Winfrey's talk show on a thirteen-inch television set perched on a small table in the corner.

The mattress, TV, and table had been donated to Khadija, along with everything else in her apartment, by the refugee resettlement agency that had helped her family start their new lives in America.

Khadija and her family were refugees from Africa, and as a volunteer, I had been helping them for several months. Khadija's husband had a full-time job, her children were thriving, she was beginning to learn English, and life was good.

Until her husband was killed in a car accident and Khadija became a young widow.

"Oprah's giving that woman a house," I explained to Khadija as we sat, side by side, on the mattress on the floor. On the screen, an excited African American woman was clapping her hands and jumping up and down as the talk show host assured her that indeed, the house was hers, and she would never have to worry about having a roof over her head again.

Khadija nodded but said nothing. When I entered the room earlier, her eyes, brimming with sadness but no tears, had met mine when I told her I was sorry to hear what had happened to her husband. I wasn't sure what else to say, as I had yet to learn about how her culture mourned the loss of loved ones.

Khadija was one of the tens of thousands of refugees known as the Somali Bantu, an oppressed and marginalized minority who fled Somalia at the onset of the civil war in the early 1990s. A decade later approximately twelve thousand Bantu were allowed to come to the United States, and several hundred settled in the town where I lived.

My initial volunteer assignment with Khadija led to a deeper and deeper connection with the Somali Bantu community, one that has lasted for twelve years.

On the day I sat with Khadija in her bedroom, unable due to our language barrier to say anything but "I'm so sorry," I never dreamed that seven years later, I, too, would become a widow.

Or that it would be the Somali Bantus' turn to look into my eyes with a sadness and understanding that crossed cultural and language differences, and say, "Oh, sorry, sorry, sorry. Your husband, he was good man."

They did not follow up their words of condolence by saying that they knew how I felt, or by recounting their own losses, as Americans so often do. They allowed the silence to sit there in the space between us, and in that silence I took comfort.

As I began reading books about grief by psychologists, social workers, and other professionals, I noticed that from time to time cultural differences regarding mourning were discussed, and I thought about my Somali Bantu friends. These were people whose losses were profound, whose villages had been raided and family members murdered in front of them—for *years*. Their babies had starved to death due to drought and lack of food. Those who were sick had died from lack of access to medicine.

If any people were "experts" on grief, they were.

On one of my return visits to my former town, I decided to ask more questions.

"I know Khadija was supposed to stay in her house after her husband died," I said to Mumina, a young Somali Bantu woman I had known (and helped raise) since she was a child. "What else can you tell me about what happens when a woman becomes a widow?"

"Yeah, the woman, she is supposed to go out only for appointments for four months," she replied. "Everyone in the community, they take care of the kid, visit her, cook for her…"

I told Mumina about my own experience of being largely alone (with the exception of one friend) in the big city where my husband died, details of which I had never shared with her before.

"If you were here, we never would have left you alone," she declared. "My mom, she would have cooked for you and we would have visited you every day."

I knew she was telling the truth. My experience of widowhood would have been vastly different had circumstances permitted me to remain in the same town. The Somali Bantu did not move to new cities unless they had a supportive network of family and friends. Survival in their African villages had depended upon it, and they brought that interdependence to America.

As soon as Khadija's husband died, the community members sprang into action. Every family in the community donated money to pay for the funeral. My friend Dadiri explained this custom to me.

"No matter how much money the woman has, she does not pay for anything," he said. "The community, we pay for the funeral, all the food for everyone who visit... everything."

"In America, the widow pays for her husband's funeral," I told him. "Maybe some relatives might help, but it's not a tradition or anything. If she's lucky, her husband bought a life insurance policy or they saved enough money to pay for it."

The day I visited Khadija, there had been a number of people in her townhouse apartment. They had waved me upstairs and when I returned, they were still there, talking amongst themselves.

"The families, they take turns," Mumina had explained. "Every day, like, two families come and sit with the woman. Maybe she sleep, but they are still there so if she wake up, she won't be sad. And she don't have to worry about her children. The other moms take care of them."

I had explained to Dadiri that I had gone to a counselor after my husband died to talk about my feelings.

He smiled and replied, "The woman in America go to counselor for everything!"

I chuckled and nodded. "Well, that's because a lot of us don't have anyone to talk to and we want to talk about our husbands. Who do the Somali Bantu widows talk to?"

Dadiri considered the question for a moment before answering. "The close family members, she can talk to them, but too much talking about the husband, it can make her sick," he said. "So we say, don't make yourself a high temper or we may lose you, too."

"A 'high temper'? What is that?"

"A high temper is when.. " he searched for the right words. "... when maybe the blood pressure goes up. The woman, she get too much upset, so we tell her to not talk, to concentrate on the children. The kid, they need her.

"And for Eid, we say the dad is not there, so who can buy those stuff?" (I knew he was referring to the clothes that were normally bought for the children during the Muslim holy days.) "The community take the place of the dad. We buy for the children. In our language it is called 'yatima.'"

Over time I have had many opportunities to reflect upon the differences between the mourning practices of my Somali Bantu friends and those of my own culture. Would I have wanted to remain secluded in my home for several months after my husband's death, had that been an option? Would I have wanted people to visit me every single day?

Perhaps not months of seclusion, and maybe not community visits *every* day, but although the specifics might differ, I appreciated the general principles of mourning that my friends subscribed to.

A widow is immediately enveloped in community. A widow does not bear the financial burden of her husband's burial or funeral expenses. A widow has support in caring for her children. On special days, she and her children are not forgotten. The community treats her with care and respect.

A widow does not experience the singular pain that isolation brings.

"There are many things I like about how your culture handles widowhood," I told my friend Dadiri. "But in my culture, we're so used to being independent that it might be hard to have people around all the time—although every few days would be nice. And as far as counseling, sometimes it's easier to talk to a stranger than people we know. I know that sounds strange, but it's true. That's why we sometimes sit around in groups with other widows and talk about our husbands."

I thought about all the death and suffering my Somali Bantu friends had endured and felt a bit embarrassed. They had rarely spoken of their losses in all the years we had spent together. They had all lost family members in the war but the idea of sitting around and talking about it would be unthinkable. It would prevent them from getting on with their lives.

For so long their cultural baseline had been day-to-day survival, not self-examination. Survival may no longer be an issue, but talking was a poor substitute for action as there were practical matters to consider. Who will the widow live with now? Will she need financial help from the community going forward? Should any of the children be given to relatives to raise? If she is younger, are there any prospects for remarriage within the community at the appropriate time?

Was their way the "healthiest" way to deal with death, especially sudden, traumatic, or violent death? Who was I—or anyone else—to say?

My friends have never heard of Elisabeth Kübler-Ross, Sigmund Freud, or any other "grief expert." They don't know a thing about stages of grief or tasks that need to be completed for healing. They have never conducted any research or studies. They just keep putting one foot in front of the other.

Which is what nearly all of us, regardless of our culture, regardless of whether or not we consult "experts," seem to do anyway.

As I was putting the finishing touches on this book, I received the devastating news of the death of a Somali Bantu man I considered a dear friend. His wife, now a widow, had once comforted me when my own husband was diagnosed with cancer. She will remain in seclusion for a few months and the community will take care of her and her minor children. Every family in the community will contribute one hundred dollars to pay for burial costs. They will do this even though most of them can barely make ends meet on wages averaging ten dollars per hour.

The women will cry with my friend, and then they will try to help her heal. She entered Grief Country a long time ago, having lost two children to starvation in Africa. Now she is experiencing Grief Country in a new way.

When I see my newly bereaved friend again, the language barrier will have no bearing on our shared sorrow. Our eyes will speak to each other, widow to widow.

I know now that my long-ago words to the other young widow, Khadija, were inadvertently the right words, the only thing I needed to say, "I'm so sorry."

I will sit with the new widow and we will talk about her children and practical matters. Her daughter will translate when needed. Other Somali Bantu neighbors will wander in and out of her apartment, shaking my hand and offering condolences about my mother's recent death, as they did when my husband died. We will shake our heads in sorrow over our mutual friend's death and the challenges facing his widow, but we will not dwell on it too long.

And I will feel as if my friend will eventually be okay, as her community surrounds her and helps her walk through her loss, a journey most of them know all too well.

When I descended into dark places at times during widowhood, I thought about my brave friends and the unspeakable tragedies they had suffered as refugees. It did not erase my own pain, but eventually it did allow a sliver of the light of perspective to permeate the darkness. Over time the sliver of light grew into a beacon. Perspective does not cancel out pain, but eventually it can help to create a sense of balance.

My friends, who are true grief experts, have taught me more than they will ever know.

THE SECOND WORST

I couldn't believe my ears.

"She's had the *second worst kind of loss you can have*," my friend was saying to another woman as we stood next to the tall round table holding our cocktails.

I felt shock and even anger course through my body as I willed myself to show absolutely no reaction to the well-intentioned but nevertheless outrageous comment about my loss.

The *second worst*? What the hell was that supposed to mean?

It meant that I had only lost a husband, not a child.

It meant that my grief was probably not as bad as it could have been.

It meant that my friend was trying to assess and rank my loss on an imaginary scale.

Comparing and judging. During the past five years, one of the things that has bothered me the most is listening to people compare and judge grief and loss.

How can you measure the depth of someone else's pain?

I know a young American woman who lost her baby a few hours after his birth. I also have a good friend, an African woman who was forced to watch her two babies starve to death before her very eyes during the civil war in Somalia.

I can't imagine saying to the American woman, "Your loss could be worse. I know a woman who lost *two* children."

When we compare and judge losses, we're being just as ridiculous and hurtful.

I am one hundred percent sure that the woman who described my loss as the "second worst" had no intention of being hurtful. In fact, I believe she was attempting to acknowledge that my loss was significant and show sympathy. She had no way of knowing that her words would be upsetting to a widow.

Unfortunately, making comparisons about losses is quite common. What are we comparing, exactly? The impact on our ability to function in a "normal" manner? The impact of a particular loss on our health? The frequency of tears or outward level of despair? What is the yardstick by which we assess whose loss is "worse"?

Those who have entered Grief Country often gravitate towards the State of Comparing Losses. It can require a conscious effort to walk away from that unhealthy place.

When my adult stepchildren lost their father, I felt terrible for them, but a voice in my head said, *My pain is worse. I lost my husband.*

I had to remind myself that I couldn't possibly know the depth of their pain. Yes, I had also lost a father, but I was not in my twenties and we had a vastly different relationship. The loss of their father was the *worst loss* of their lives thus far. Period. Might other, even more painful losses follow? Quite possibly, but that was irrelevant. I could not allow the pain of my own loss to prevent me from giving them one hundred percent empathy and support for their loss.

My friend's implication that losing a child is "worse" than losing a spouse may very well be true—and my instinctive reaction that my loss of a husband was "worse" than the loss of a parent may also be true. However, if we continue to measure degrees of grief by relationship, we do an injustice to the unmarried, childless woman whose mother was her closest friend. And we don't take into account the woman who grieves the loss of her loyal best friend since childhood more than the loss of her chronically unfaithful and abusive husband.

There are those who believe a spouse's sudden, unexpected death is worse than a slow, excruciating one, or that a woman who was a devoted "partner" or "significant other" for twenty years suffers less than one who was legally married.

All these comparisons! What do they accomplish?

Their only purpose seems to be to give us reasons to withhold to some degree our acknowledgment and validation of others' losses.

There is another aspect of comparing losses that widows encounter. In an early draft of this book, I initially included this observation in the chapter entitled, "Anger," because there are few things that infuriate a widow more than the lack of understanding about this:

A *non-death loss* is not the same as a *death loss.*

I am not talking about "better" or "worse" here. I am speaking of the frequency with which some women *equate* experiencing divorce or other losses in their lives with widowhood.

I have personally been told by several women that they knew exactly how I felt because they had gone through a painful divorce.

I was even told by a woman who had been unemployed for an extended period of time that it was the same thing as being a widow.

Many, if not most, widows have heard similar comments. A husband who travels a lot is equated with the husband who died. Children leaving home for college are equated with the husband who died. A house lost for economic reasons is equated with the husband who died.

Divorce and other non-death losses are real and painful—sometimes excruciatingly painful. Many of the "secondary losses" that widows experience, such as financial losses, relationships that disappear, etc., are shared by women who are divorced. The practical issues of rebuilding one's life may be similar in many ways. There can certainly be overwhelming emotions involved.

But make no mistake: *A non-death loss is not the* **same** *as a death loss.*

If divorce is the same as widowhood, why don't widows say to divorced women, "I know exactly how you feel. I'm a widow." It doesn't happen. It never will happen. Yet the reverse happens all too frequently.

Widows have an incredible amount of self-restraint. A widow may hear these remarks and not react. She may feel as if a knife has been plunged into her heart, yet she will not respond in kind. She will not say to her married friend, *You don't have the slightest idea what you're talking about. Your husband will come back from his extended trip. Mine won't. Being lonely for two weeks does not give you any insight whatsoever into widowhood.* Nor will she say to a divorced friend, *He may have broken your heart but your ex-husband is alive. You didn't bury him and you don't have to explain to your children that they will never, ever, see their daddy again. Do you know how much you are hurting me when you say such things?*

Instead, widows will remain silent or share their pain with other widows.

And sometimes a widow will look back upon her life and wonder if she ever hurt another widow by diminishing her loss in this way. She may wonder how often she compared losses or withheld empathy. It's not uncommon to visit the State of Humility when we reflect upon our own past failings in this regard.

Comparisons and judgments about the loss can sometimes creep into efforts to "console" a widow.

I knew one widow who attended a wedding a year after her husband's death. One of his friends from college offered condolences, then remarked, "Well, what did you expect when you married such an old guy?"

He felt free to judge and attempt to diminish her grief.

I listened as one widow whose husband died from lung cancer expressed her anger over the frequency with which folks asked if he had been a smoker. What is the point of asking a widow that question? Her husband is dead. She is grieving. She doesn't need the judgment that is contained in that question.

Consoling a widow can, admittedly, be difficult. Widowhood can feel as if your entire body is covered by an emotional sunburn, and when someone says "the wrong thing" (which is different things to different widows), it can feel like a brutal slap to the reddened, raw layer of grief that covers your skin for weeks, months, and sometimes longer.

The comments that actually *did* console me were never comments that compared my loss to other types of losses or contained judgments about my loss. Those comments only stoked indignation and even anger.

Many people are tempted to point out factors they believe will mitigate a widow's grief.

The following chart illustrates my take on why this might not be helpful:

Objective Fact	Common Assumption	Widow's Subjective Feelings
They had 40 happy years together.	All those memories should lessen her pain.	Pain.
He was a smoker.	She should not have been surprised by his death so her pain should be less.	Pain.
They were married only 2 years.	She's young and she'll find love again so her pain should be less.	Pain.
He was sick for a long time.	She's already grieved so her grief should be less.	Pain.
He is dead.		Pain -- but eventually she will experience less pain, an ability to function normally (most of the time), a healthy re-engagement with life, perhaps even gratitude for time they had.

Eventually a widow will feel less pain, but it will have nothing to do with someone pointing out objective facts regarding her husband's death to her.

But won't pointing out objective facts give a widow "perspective" and thereby diminish her grief?

Most widows eventually find a place for perspective in their lives, but from what I've observed and experienced, perspective rarely comes from the efforts of another person to foist it upon us. Frankly, those efforts are usually dismissed out of hand because in the eyes of many widows, an unwidowed person simply lacks credibility on this issue. Even a fellow widow cannot know when perspective will become meaningful again to another widow.

And the common assumptions about how objective facts will lessen a widow's grief are usually just flat-out wrong. My husband was sick for more than a year before he died. It was an objective fact that I had time to get used to the idea of his death. Did that make his death easier? No. Living with a horrifying prospect for many months does not lessen the pain of having that horrifying prospect realized.

In Grief Country, relief from the fresh psychological pain of widowhood is not usually found in the State of Intellectualizing.

When it comes to consoling a widow, taking time to learn "what to say" to a griever can seem burdensome.

I recall the time a relative visited my mother, who had Alzheimer's disease. He was clearly uncomfortable upon seeing that the disease had progressed and my mother was no longer able to interact as easily as she had during a previous visit. After the visit, I thought it might be helpful to provide a handout that listed tips for visiting an individual with Alzheimer's.

My relative never came to visit my mother again.

Even though a widow's situation is obviously different, I can't help but wonder if the same principle applies: in general, people don't want or don't have time for "homework" of this nature.

Some widows aren't bothered by any of the things people say in an effort to comfort them, but many others are. Since there's no way to know how comments will be received, my own advice about what to say to a widow would simply be this: don't use platitudes, don't start sentences with "at least," and don't use her grief as a jumping off point for telling your own story. Please be sensitive to the subject of faith or religion. It's a normal response to grief to question one's faith and the values one previously held. Let this process play out on the widow's own timetable and on her terms.

Instead, use words that simply acknowledge her loss.

"I can't imagine how you must be feeling."

"The future must seem so overwhelming to you right now."

And one will never go wrong with:

"Do you want to talk? I have plenty of time to listen."

In Grief Country, I've tried to avoid the State of Comparing Losses and Judging in favor of the State of Consoling. Those who choose to enter this state should bring suitcases stuffed with humility, empathy, and patience, and be prepared to stay awhile. You will be a welcome guest.

A MOMENT OF SILENCE

We live in a world where people pause for a moment of silence to remember the departed. A moment, not an hour, or a day. Then we throw out that first pitch, or we hand out those diplomas, or we present those awards.

Life goes on.

In her private box seat, a widow does not hear the roar of the crowd as the ballplayer hits a home run in the first inning. It may take months for it to even register that a ball game is being played in front of her on the field.

She is frozen in that initial moment of silence.

It is a surreal feeling. A widow knows that there has always been pain and death in the world, that there is "nothing new under the sun," as the Teacher said in the Book of Ecclesiastes, but knowing it intellectually does nothing to prepare her for knowing it in her very being as the fog of widowhood seeps into her brain and her body shakes and shudders from the trauma of losing her other half.

I had no idea that a person could endure so much pain without actually dying.

How can the rest of the world go on so blithely? a widow wonders. At first "the rest of the world" is comprised of those around her who are not dealing with the upheaval of a death loss. They are out and about, enjoying their lives.

Then she watches the news and realizes just how much suffering actually exists in "the rest of the world" outside her small sphere.

For a while the news of catastrophic events in the rest of the world can seem intensely personal. After my husband died, I watched news coverage of an earthquake in India and burst into tears, thinking about the women who had suddenly become widows and the children who were now fatherless. I cried at the reports of soldiers lost in Iraq or Afghanistan. Any story of death loss affected me deeply. I felt as if I was some kind of grief sponge, soaking up all the tears of the world.

Over time this feeling of overwhelming empathy-on-steroids faded.

A person can only sustain this type of deep emotion for so long. We are not wired to be in a constant state of distress. Eventually equilibrium finds its way back into a widow's psyche, but those who care about a widow would do well to understand this phenomenon. It is not her fault if she comes across as "over the top" or "extreme" in her reactions long after the official "moment of silence" has been observed. The luggage she is dragging around Grief Country can become unbearably heavy as she piles other people's pain on top of her own.

This chapter is being written on the heels of a seemingly unprecedented series of tragedies and natural disasters: Hurricane Harvey, Hurricane Irma, Hurricane Maria, the massacre of innocents in Las Vegas, and the devastating wildfires in California.

Hundreds dead, towns and even entire islands destroyed, infrastructure ripped to shreds, lives in ruin.

Watching the news reports of each individual catastrophe made an indelible impression on me. Weeks later, however, it became difficult to remember… Was Hurricane Irma the one that affected Texas or Florida? How many people actually lost their lives in the wildfire? Was it hundreds or was that Las Vegas?

The tragedies happened in such rapid succession that the "moment of silence" truly did seem to be just a moment for many of us who were safely on the outside.

I was in my fifth year of widowhood and although I felt terrible for the victims, I no longer had that "empathy-on-steroids" feeling that had characterized my first year or so of widowhood. Their losses receded into the back of my mind—far too soon.

Similarly, when I lost my husband, although it was my personal Hurricane Maria, there were other calamities making headlines in the lives of those around me. I shouldn't have been surprised that the moment of silence about my loss seemed to be, indeed, just a moment. How much attention could they pay to my hurricane?

Most widows I know want to talk about their late husbands. And talk and talk and talk. To this day I could easily spend several hours detailing what an old-fashioned gentleman my husband was. I have had to learn how to read others' expressions—even those who are receptive to my bringing up my husband—to gauge when I've talked about him too much, when I've made them a bit uncomfortable, when I need to retreat back into silence.

My loss was acknowledged for a moment in time. I had to learn to be satisfied with that moment.

And not begrudge those who quickly turned their attention back to the ball game.

Metamorphosis
(Written in Year Five)

** Inseparable * Intertwined **
** Indescribable * Incomparable **
** Irreplaceable **
Unforeseen
Unspeakable
Unfathomable
Unraveled
Unmoored
Unimportant
Uninvited
Unseen
Unheard
Unnoticed
Indignant Undefeated Inspired Unflinching
Invincible Unbowed Indestructible
Unapologetic Indomitable Unshakable
Unstoppable
WIDOW

SOCIAL MEDIA

To say I was late to join the world of social media is an understatement. When Facebook became popular, one of my stepchildren tried to explain it to my husband and me. We looked at each other, mystified. Why on earth would we spend time sitting at the computer and putting pictures of ourselves "out there" just so other people could know what we were doing? Why would they care? And why would we be interested in what other people were doing? Isn't that why you visit them once in a great while, to "catch up" and then be on your way? We just didn't see the point.

During the last few months of my husband's life, we finally set up a Facebook page so he could see photos of his relatives. We posted a few pictures—mostly old memories—but his illness soon caused him to lose interest. As for me, I was unprepared for how I would be affected by seeing photos of other people "having fun" and enjoying their lives while my husband's life was ending and my world was collapsing all around me.

I deleted the Facebook page as soon as he passed away.

My second foray into Facebook was not quite as short-lived, but it eventually became clear to me that I could not handle unexpectedly seeing photos of my husband, especially ones where he was sick. What might have been a good memory to one person was to me a trigger to remember all the things that had happened that day, including difficulties known only to me.

Once again social media proved to be too much for me. And the same feeling of disconnection between the lives of others and my own life was still there, perhaps magnified even more now that I was a widow.

When a widow is in deep grief, it can also be jarring to see certain photos—posted by online friends—of people in hospital beds, perhaps receiving cancer treatment. I often cried after viewing images of these individuals (especially the children), even though I did not know them personally. In addition to triggering my "empathy-on-steroids" response, these pictures would trigger memories of my husband's cancer battle.

When I saw a grief counselor two years after my husband died, she said, "I have a lot of widowed clients who stopped using Facebook. It was affecting their mental health." Like me, they found it too upsetting for one reason or another.

Social media can be a double-edged sword for a widow. On the one hand, it definitely helped me to be away from it so that I could focus on my own healing and my own life, but on the other hand, I was unable to avail myself of the connections that could be found online with other widows via "Facebook groups" and other social media. I was in my third year of widowhood before I took another plunge into social media and discovered an online group of widows encouraging other widows. What a difference that connection would have made to me had I been aware of it during my first or second year of widowhood, when I was feeling so isolated!

It can be perplexing to try to understand the "rules" of social media when one is a widow. I rarely post pictures of my husband, but I have heard of widows who are criticized for posting "too many" pictures of their late husbands. (People might not understand that the intention is not to remind them of a widow's suffering but to honor the memory of the husband and ensure they are not forgotten.)

That's part of what makes the private online groups so popular with widows. We can share memories, special days, and be ourselves, hopefully without judgment.

But even that aspect of social media can be problematic. There are privacy concerns, as those seeking vulnerable women might gain access to the group. A widow also needs to be prepared for the responses she receives to anything she posts. Although most widows post supportive or encouraging comments, sometimes the comments are not helpful. I joined one online widows' group only to leave the group two weeks later, as I quickly discovered it was basically dominated by a few widows who commented on every post. A widow needs to ask herself if she will find this interaction more irritating than helpful. As with any social media site, it's a risk when you expose your innermost thoughts and experiences to those you have never met in person.

It's important to know who is administering a private online group. Is it a nonprofit organization? A religious one? An individual who may be seeking paying clients for a service they are offering? Does a "closed" or "secret" group mean a widow's name will absolutely not be given and/or sold to those who want to sell services to widows? (It's not that difficult to obtain addresses these days, unfortunately, especially when many widows list their hometowns on their Facebook pages.)

The comments posted by widows online truly underline the diversity of widow experiences, from the women who are able to immediately embrace joy and gratitude for their lives after their husbands' deaths (yes, these widows do exist) to the women who, after many years of widowhood, still struggle mightily to adjust to the way their lives and relationships have changed.

I visit these pages sparingly, but overall, I've found them to be a helpful source of support and validation. It's also rewarding when I can find the right words to lift up another widow during a difficult time.

Deciding upon the extent to which she will be involved with social media—a seemingly benign pastime that can have a significant impact on her mental health—is yet another one of the challenges a widow faces after she enters Grief Country.

RESEARCH HAS SHOWN...

I've never been one to accept things at face value. When I read sentences that begin with, "Research has shown..." I always want to know, What research? Who conducted it and where? Was it based on case studies or surveys? How many individuals were sampled? Were the results duplicated in a later study?

Since this was my attitude *before* I became a widow, it stood to reason that in widowhood I would question what "research has shown" about grief.

Some of those who conducted research in the early days of the study of grief were later criticized for their methods. For example, grievers were interviewed only once and sample sizes were considered inadequate. In the case of Erich Lindemann's pioneering study in 1944, the lack of statistical analysis was noted, as well as the fact that the individuals he studied were not truly representative of those who were bereaved. Even Freud acknowledged shortcomings in his paper, "Mourning and Melancholia," stating, "In the opening remarks of this paper I admitted that the empirical material upon which this study is founded does not supply all we could wish."

As noted earlier, regarding Elisabeth Kübler-Ross's "five stages of grief" theory, the research that she did conduct was misapplied. Although she interviewed hundreds of people and developed detailed case studies, the individuals in question were not those who were bereaved but those who were dying. She did not conduct any research on those who were grieving a death, but the general public still assumes that her popular theory was backed up by research.

Grief experts have assured us that research methods have become more sophisticated over the past few decades, and I certainly believe that's the case. Attempting to read summaries of research conducted in recent years, containing references to "combinatoric analysis," "optimum diagnostic algorithms," and "differential item functioning analysis" was enough to make my head spin. I had to take it on faith that the methods were above reproach.

Yet even the experts acknowledge the difficulty of assessing grief. "The essential question is how to measure grief in any meaningful sense." Authors Robert O. Hansson, Bruce N. Carpenter, and Sharon K. Fairchild made that observation in their article, "Measurement Issues in Bereavement."[1]

Nearly everyone who conducts grief research has a different focus. Some measure a griever's general reactions to a death at different points in time; some measure the ability to function; some measure reactions based on type of death or other specific aspects of the loss.

The invisible grief czar has yet to come up with a study that measures all the aspects of grief in a gigantic cross-section of grievers.

It's difficult for me to imagine how those conducting grief research can control for all the dozens if not hundreds of factors that can impact a widow's reaction to her husband's death. Do all the participants in the study have the same basic personalities (seeing the glass as half full versus half empty, for example); the same backgrounds as far as how they handled previous losses; the same concurrent stressors (are they all parents of young children or caregivers for elderly parents); the same support system; the same quality of relationship with the deceased spouse prior to the death; the same current health status? Are they in the same financial situation, and did their spouses die in the same manner (unexpectedly versus after a long illness)?

There are just so many variables beyond amount of time since the death, length of marriage, and other factors that as a widow, I regard as almost irrelevant. Why? Because I've met lots of widows whose shared circumstances vis-à-vis those factors haven't necessarily translated into shared grief experiences.

And how can a researcher parse out what a widow is grieving about, specifically? Because it's never "just" the loss of the husband.

Before I joined a grief support group offered by a local nonprofit organization, an intake interview was required. I was asked whether I was grieving my husband's death, which had occurred two years earlier, or grieving the possible impending death of my mother, who had Alzheimer's disease. When I told the gentleman I was grieving "everything," he explained that he was just trying to figure out which group would best fit my needs. Nevertheless, it was impossible to answer his question.

"Concurrent stressors" and "secondary losses" were—in my mind—not separate from "grief." I had to wonder how they could be separate in the minds of the individuals who are checking off the boxes on surveys.

Do current research methods take this into account?

The average person does not usually read the medical or psychology journals that publish these studies.

Even if we do, we are not in a position to judge the validity of the research. We can't gauge whether the results were impacted by "the wording effect" (order of questions or choice of words used) or "overgeneralizing" from an insufficient sample size, or any of the other issues that good researchers try to avoid.

The average person seems to become aware of new findings only if the study produces results that prompt a mainstream article or book (which is how the discredited theory of "the five stages of grief" spread like wildfire). We read the headlines and don't ask too many questions. We just assume the research is solid unless someone on a morning talk show happens to add a caveat to the headline.

Inevitably, we make a lot of assumptions based on our own observations.

In the chapter entitled, "A Show of Hands," I described a situation in which I observed 90 percent of widows present at the same function raising their hands when asked a specific question: *Have you ever considered suicide?* From a research perspective, those widows were not a true representative sample of widows. Widows who had no impetus to attend that particular meeting, perhaps because their social and emotional support needs were being met by others, might not have raised their hands in response to the question about suicide.

Even though this book is filled with my observations and experiences, the same principle applies. I have conducted no "valid research."

Over the past few decades, attempts to measure grief have led to a variety of instruments, many focused on determining whether an individual's grief is abnormal. These include the Texas Inventory of Grief (which assesses normal versus pathological grief), the Inventory of Complicated Grief (assesses complicated grief), the Grief Intensity Scale (assesses risk of developing prolonged grief disorder), and the Grief Experience Inventory, just to name a few.

Many assessments of grief are based on self-reporting, which is by definition subjective. I personally found my journey through grief to be so unpredictable at times that a question I might have answered confidently one day would be answered a completely different way the following week—and still differently the week after that. Again, as a layperson I have to take it on faith that these types of assessments take into account similar variations in widows' responses.

I'm also curious as to when a particular assessment was developed.

During one grief support meeting I attended, the social worker who was facilitating the meeting handed out copies of the Holmes and Rahe stress scale exercise,[2] which was *designed to assess an individual's likelihood of a serious change in their health in the next year* (not measure the depth of anyone's grief). The other widows and I dutifully circled each life event that had occurred in the previous 18 to 24 months, as well as the factors that would reduce or increase stress resistance. Our scores were calculated and mine was a whopping 571 units. A score of 300 and above was supposed to indicate an 80 percent chance of a serious change in health.

Losing a spouse was rated as 100 units, but many widows also experience the attendant stressors of "change in financial state" (38 units), "change in social activities" (18 units), etc. A widow could conceivably amass several hundred points in the first section of the exercise.

I recalled a grief workshop I attended immediately after my husband's death, in which I learned that illness was quite common in the first year of widowhood. Having some rationale for that statement was important to me, so I appreciated learning about the stress scale.

But was the assessment up to date?

When I noted that the stress scale was developed in 1967, I was a bit skeptical. However, I discovered that its validity was tested in a subsequent study in 1970 and again in a study done by Cornell University. Thousands of individuals had been questioned and factors like cultural differences were taken into account. Care had obviously been taken to avoid overgeneralizing from an inadequate sample of participants or only certain segments of the population.

As for my subjective findings, I did not have a significant change in my *physical* health during the following year; however, my mental health suffered to the point where it became critical for me to seek one-on-one counseling.

What about the questions themselves? As I perused the Holmes and Rahe stress scale, I thought about the "life events" that were listed and contemplated how much society has changed since 1967. In 1967 we were in the middle of the Vietnam War, with several wars to follow. Surely "Returned to America from war zone" would rate as a stressful life event? Or "Survived mass shooting" or "Survived terrorist attack" (something that is tragically becoming more commonplace)? Today a stressful life event might be "Became target of cyber-bullying." What about "Began new life as a refugee"? Based on the years I spent helping refugees start new lives in the United States, I would definitely assign this life event a score of 100.

While these observations don't directly connect to widowhood, my point is that we should always be questioning the instruments used in "research," both past and present. And we need to know more about what findings support the latest theories and headlines about grief before we accept them wholesale.

It's not that easy for the average person to access articles in medical or psychology journals. Internet resources such as Google Scholar do not necessarily provide complete articles. For example, in order to obtain a full-length copy of Erich Lindemann's "Symptomology and Management of Acute Grief," I had three choices. I could pay around $40 to have a copy sent to me, I could pay hundreds of dollars for a journal subscription that would entitle me to access the full text, or I could visit the library of the nearby state university to access this journal and the others that I reference in this book.

I opted to go to the university and merely pay for parking.

While traveling Grief Country, some widows never set foot in the State of Research. They are far too busy visiting the other states, or they may be satisfied with souvenirs, taking for granted that whatever information is given to them truly came from that state. Whoever travels there, however, should exercise caution as they explore the area.

I haven't spent nearly as much time in the State of Research as I'd like to, but at this point in my life I am running out of time to plan many more trips.

Still, it's an important part of Grief Country.

PSST! TELL YOUR FRIEND!

Dear Kate,

I really appreciate our long friendship, and I'm thankful it continued after my husband died.

I've been thinking a lot lately about some important things I'd like to pass on about widowhood... oh, not to you, of course, but to your friend, Mary.

I know none of this will apply to you. You have a plan in place, after all. You and your husband are going to pass away in your nineties, lying in bed peacefully, holding hands.* You are certainly not going to be one of the 700,000-or-so women who become widows every year.

But I am concerned Mary might be one of them. And I'd like her to know some things that no one ever told me about widowhood.

For readers who may think I am being snarky, I am not. When my great-grandparents died within mere days of each other, it was such an unusual occurrence that it was in the local newspaper under the headline: "Follows Her Aged Husband to Grave."

Would you mind telling her how incredibly important it is to have a few practical things in place?

Like life insurance, for example.

Oh, my gosh, how I needed the modest life insurance policy my husband had maintained since he was in his twenties. His illness had prompted withdrawals from our retirement accounts that hadn't been foreseen. Without life insurance, I'm not sure how I would have made it through that first year of widowhood.

I know your friend Mary hasn't worked outside the home for a while. She may not realize how difficult it will be for her to find a job if her husband dies. Age discrimination is real and her resume might not get her very far. She's going to need a safety net.

For the cost of dinner out at a restaurant one night a month, a premium might be paid on a life insurance policy and Mary might be able to have a little peace of mind. She sure doesn't want to be one of the approximately 40 percent of women whose husbands have no life insurance in place!

Now I know you and your husband don't need to do any end-of-life planning, given that you're going to pass away at the same time, but Mary really should make sure she and her husband have these advance planning tools in place:

> An *Advance Directive*, which consists of two documents:

1) A *Health Care Directive*, which states an individual's wishes regarding which life-sustaining measures and/or medical interventions they would/would not want in the event they are incapacitated and unable to communicate their wishes.

2) A *Durable Power of Attorney for Health Care* (also known as Medical Power of Attorney),

which appoints a Health Care Agent who will ensure the instructions in the Health Care Directive are followed if an individual is incapacitated and unable to speak for themselves.

➤ In the case of progressive or chronic illness, a *POLST* form—completed with and signed by a doctor—should be posted where emergency medical personnel can access it.

➤ A Will and/or any Trust Documents

➤ A Financial Power of Attorney may be needed.

➤ Additional documents appropriate to the circumstances and prepared by an attorney.

Mary should discuss her husband's wishes regarding any type of funeral or "celebration of life" and, if possible, write those wishes down. Sadly, there are individuals or even family members who will think nothing of criticizing a grieving widow about everything from the obituary to the funeral or memorial service, even if she is honoring her husband's wishes. Death can bring out some true ugliness of character.

While doing research for a speech I gave once about Alzheimer's, I was surprised to learn that seven out of ten elderly persons will need long-term care. So even if Mary and her husband reach old age together, there's a distinct possibility that if they do not have long-term care insurance, their financial resources might have to be used for *his* care, since women generally outlive men. I've met quite a few widows who, like me, are now worried about how they will pay for their *own* medical treatment or long-term care after paying for their husband's care. Mary needs to give some thought to how to protect her assets from being depleted this way.

There are documents that Mary will need to put her hands on quickly if her husband dies. As I recall, you told me he was a veteran. I don't know if she might want him to be buried in a veterans' cemetery, but she will need to have his discharge papers (Form DD-214). She should ask her husband where these papers are while he's still alive, because the last thing she will want to be doing is searching through the attic for his military papers!

She will need some information for her husband's death certificate that one might not normally think about, such as his parents' full names (including his mother's full name before her first marriage) and the city he was born in.

She should also make sure she has some other documents located and on hand: their marriage certificate, his birth certificate, even his divorce decree from his first marriage (yes, she might need to provide this for certain benefits, such as the Veterans Administration's Aid and Attendance program). She will need to know the locations of titles to their vehicles, the deed to their house, copies of recent income tax returns, and the keys to their safe deposit box, if they have one.

I know you and Mary go shopping a lot and you've told me how she can go a little crazy with her credit cards! She might want to make sure that her name is on the cards she wants to keep. When my husband died, there was a credit card that was in his name only. I'm not sure how the bank found out so quickly that he had died, but within two weeks I had received a letter from them saying they would appreciate the balance being paid off so they could close the account! They did not offer a card to me. Fortunately, I had other cards with my name on them, but still… it hadn't even occurred to me that my available credit could change so quickly upon my husband's death.

Speaking of credit cards, does Mary know everything her husband knows about their finances? Because she needs to! I can't tell you how many widows lament, "Joe used to handle all that," or "I only paid the monthly bills, so I didn't know anything about our investments." Now is the time, while he's healthy, for Mary's husband to sit down with her and go over any 401(k) retirement accounts, pensions—all their assets and liabilities, actually. And he needs to share any advice he has for her. I remember after my husband died, a financial advisor told me he'd "take the place" of my husband in helping me with financial matters. A month later I was several thousand dollars poorer, due to his advice! So Mary needs to educate herself and be wary of all those who will gladly descend upon her in widowhood to "help" her with her finances. Make sure she asks them the question: Is he or she going to act in a "fiduciary" capacity? A fiduciary has the highest legal duty to act in the client's best interest, rather than to try to sell her investment products that will earn them a commission but are not in her best interest or suited to her investment objectives and risk tolerance.

Now, practical matters such as these have their place, but there's another subject Mary might want to consider: Who has a "duty of care" for her in the event that her husband passes away? From what you've told me, Mary's family is scattered around the country, although she does have a number of local friends. Even if Mary thinks a number of these individuals do have an obligation to ensure her health and well-being, do they feel the same way?

Mary also might want to think about how her family and friends have dealt with previous losses. It may give her an inkling as to how they might deal with her loss, should it occur.

Does she know any widows? Because there will come a time when she will want to share something that only another widow will understand.

There's no way Mary can know for certain how any one individual might react to her becoming a widow, so it wouldn't be a bad idea for her to start being realistic about her support network and try to strengthen it whenever she can. Please tell her not to be shocked if some of her friends or family suddenly turn into "Houdini" and disappear for a while. It happens.

There is a limit to what a wife can do to "prepare" for widowhood, but I hope passing along a few of these thoughts might be helpful to Mary. The most important thing, of course, is that Mary cherish each and every moment she has with her husband. If he passes away, all the little things that get on her nerves today will be irritations she would give anything to have to deal with once again. Tell her to create as many memories as she can, every day.

Oh, one more thing. I know you've said Mary's husband isn't exactly a romantic, but *please* try to get him to write Mary a love letter—not a few lines in a Hallmark card, but an actual letter. It doesn't have to be flowery or too mushy and the spelling and grammar don't matter... just tell him to pour his love for Mary into every word. She will cherish it forever and it will keep her going through her darkest hours.

Thanks in advance, Kate, for sharing my thoughts with Mary, and have a wonderful anniversary trip with your husband. I wish you many, many more happy years!

Love, Stephanie

EXPERTS (PART 2)

What could I learn about grief from the "experts"? That was one of the questions I set out to answer after my husband died. Could I acquire information that would lessen my grief? Or at least allow me to better understand it?

The answers to the latter two questions were "no" and "yes."

Nothing I read in the experts' books and journal articles lessened my grief—unless one could factor in the "break from grief" that took place while I was immersing myself in studying their theories. In fact, it was rather disconcerting, in the beginning, to discover that even those who had studied grief for decades did not have a mutually agreed-upon, definitive answer about the nature and course of grief—especially when they stated their *individual* views so definitively!

The heartache I lived with every day could not be chased away by intellectual reasoning, research, or statistics.

But the desire I had for "understanding" *could* be satisfied to a great degree by intellectual reasoning, research, and statistics. I could read the various theories and apply them to my own experience. Take anticipatory grief, for example. Learning about the reactions that have been noted among those whose loved ones are dying completely changed my understanding of an incredibly difficult time in my life (albeit after the fact). Without the work of the experts in documenting and analyzing this type of grief, I wouldn't have been able to process this period of my life in the way that I—a person who likes to mentally organize my experiences—needed to process it.

Without studying grief theories throughout the years, I might not have known that there were other theories beyond Elisabeth Kübler-Ross's "five stages" theory (such as the "dual process" theory). I might have accepted without question the declarative statements that many individuals, especially individuals who are perceived to be in positions of authority, made about grief.

As I learned more, however, I began noticing how many erroneous statements were being put forth. At times it's been a challenge not to speak up, to say, "Well, no, that's actually not true," but putting a person in a perceived position of authority on the spot usually does not endear a widow to them, so I've seldom said anything.

The answer to all this confusion, in my view, is not to argue with those who have not studied grief to any great extent. Rather, the answer is to encourage widows to become their own grief experts. Does that mean a widow needs to find a copy of Erich Lindemann's seminal article from 1944 about grief? No. It just means that widows need to use discernment in deciding whether or not to accept that what a person in authority or another widow is telling them about their experience of grief is accurate or true for them.

The internet is full of outdated and unsubstantiated articles and blog posts about grief that might appear at the top of a Google search, not necessarily due to their accuracy, but by virtue of having the right "search engine optimization" keywords. One simple thing a widow can do is scroll to the end of an article and check to see whether any references have been listed. If she does this, she will soon start recognizing which experts are the most credible sources for information.

When I visited a number of bookstores that featured used books, the sections on "grief" contained few, if any, scholarly works. Instead, there were usually worn copies of Kübler-Ross's *On Death and Dying* as well as a few books by other popular authors who are not considered "experts" in the sense of writing scholarly tomes. The books on these shelves were easy to read and undoubtedly helpful to many individuals, but they were not the same as academic works. Obviously, that's why theories such as the "five stages theory" continue to be accepted as fact. The scholarly experts—the psychologists and psychiatrists who publish their findings in journals primarily read by their peers—need to figure out a way to educate the public in a way that's more easily accessible to grievers.

Over the past five years, I haven't taken offense if a few of those who live in Grief Country have alerted me to hazardous roads or dangerous terrain, or if they have shared tips about where they found restful territory. I've occasionally needed help with carrying all my baggage, the kind of expert help that I found from counseling, for example.

I learned early on that sometimes the directions given to me were faulty, and I had to study the map and decide which route through Grief Country would work best for me on my individual journey.

I now consider myself to be a "grief expert"—an expert on my *own* grief, no one else's. For me, becoming my own grief expert merely means that I have empowered myself to own my grief, understand it as clearly as possible, and not let anyone else have authority or control over it.

An "expert" is defined as one who has "authoritative knowledge" about a subject. I would give anything not to be an expert when it comes to grief, but I've spent far too much time in Grief Country for that to be possible. I can't pretend I do not know this terrain like the back of my hand.

When it comes to grief, there are a lot of experts. Experts in research. Experts in devising theories that explain human behavior in conjunction with that research. Experts in helping grievers through the unbearable and unimaginable in a multitude of ways. Experts in defining the nature and course of the various paths that grief can take.

I respect the widow who is an expert in dealing with grief while raising small children. I am in awe of the elderly widow who is an expert in finding reasons to go on when her husband and all her peers have passed away. I honor the experts who know the singular pain of losing a husband who was serving his country. The list could go on and on, so diverse are our individual experiences in processing our grief.

So many experts in Grief Country. It is a strange land, one with no king, no president, no chief executive officer. We are all experts and all equals here.

THE CHAIN
(Written in Year Four)

Knock ever so softly
on the door of my heart
I will not turn you away
but I cannot let you in

You may reach for my hand
through the chain on the door
Press a memory into my palm
Glance fleetingly past me
into this sacred room
A million square feet of pure devotion

How I long to fling the door open
arms outstretched
but I would crash violently to the floor
The blood of my grief would splatter
across my freshly painted walls

The window overlooking the garden
I planted only last year
would shatter into a thousand shards of glass
piercing the veil of denial I don each day
like a suit of armor

Knock ever so gently
on the door of my heart
I will not turn you away
But I dare not let you in

Forgive me and know—
It cost me all I once was
all we once were
To fashion this tourniquet
To save my own life
To put the chain on the door

BUILDING BRIDGES

I was feeling overwhelmed. Two moves within the year prior to my husband's death had created confusion when it came to locating certain items, such as the tools I needed to make minor home repairs. Even if I could locate the drill I was looking for, I wasn't too confident about my ability to use it.

"Ron used to handle all of this stuff," I complained in frustration to my friend, who had arrived with her tool box and experience in home maintenance.

"Well, now you know what it's like to be single," she responded bluntly.

I was stunned. And deeply hurt. And a bit incredulous. Surely my never-married friend wasn't equating widowhood to being single?

I said nothing. The home repairs were completed and my friend left.

I burst into tears.

My friend is a wonderful person. She would never intentionally hurt anyone. I knew she had not intended to hurt me with her off-the-cuff remark.

She just didn't "get it."

My complaints about my husband not being there to handle home repairs were not merely about that issue. My words were reflective of the overwhelming pain I was feeling, the grief that was still encapsulating my body, the fear that I was not up to the challenge of living life on my own, the lingering feeling of unfairness that he had been taken away, and the still-present horror of watching him slowly die.

It wasn't about not being able to use a drill.

A year passed, during which time I wrote my poems and essays and read my grief books. My friend continued to be my friend, helping me until her own personal responsibilities took her out of my life for a time. By the time we reconnected again, I had figured a few things out.

I told her how affected I had been by her comment, "Now you know what it's like to be single."

She had no idea that her offhand comment had been so hurtful.

"I know you didn't mean to be unkind," I said to her. "But I do think there was a reason you said what you said. You've never been married, you've always been on your own, and maybe there were times when it was really difficult... and there I was, married, with someone to turn to for help..."

She nodded her head. "You seemed to have it pretty easy there for a while. I couldn't even get my brothers to help me with stuff. I had to do everything on my own or hire someone."

"Right," I said. "And how often did I think about you and what you might be going through? I mean, of course I thought about you, but did I really understand? Had I forgotten how hard it was for me during the years I was single?"

We talked and talked. I did my best to convey to her the depth of the pain that widowhood had created. I shared with her all the other hurtful things that had been said to me and other widows I knew.

"It's like someone is kicking you when you're down," I told her. "Casual remarks that might not bother you so much later on feel like body blows when you're grieving at first. And even if there's some truth in it, you feel like, *Really? You're saying this to me **now**?*"

I also talked about comparisons. "I don't feel 'single,' even though technically I guess I am. I still feel married. I don't have any biological kids, but I would never say that a woman who lost her child and I are both 'childless' in the same way."

My friend nodded, and shared more of her feelings about her own challenges as well as the challenge of not knowing how to handle my grief.

Our frank discussion was a turning point in our relationship. The tension that had been present for a long time began to fade. The next year another good friend of hers became a widow.

"I'm doing better with her than I did with you," my friend told me, "... doing more listening and not trying to get her to just recover as soon as possible." By this time I was able to laugh. "Lucky for *her*," I said with a trace of sarcasm. "Glad I could help!"

I learned many lessons from this experience with my friend, beginning with the realization that a hurtful remark could actually be a catalyst for increasing understanding.

I learned that it was important to identify who was open to having a conversation, and who wasn't. I knew my friend genuinely wanted to become more supportive. There were those with whom I had broached the subject of how it feels to be a widow who had immediately signaled their lack of interest in the subject. Most widows can quickly sense the unspoken words, *What's so special about **you**? Everyone has problems.*

I learned that communication would only be possible if I were willing to step back from my own situation and consider the other person's situation. Even if someone is willing to sit and listen, is it fair to place the burden of your pain upon them if they cannot take it on emotionally? Many simply can't.

Conveying one's pain in a way that doesn't make the other person feel defensive is also crucial. And I learned that an attitude of humility about one's own failure to acknowledge others' pain in the past can go a long way.

Ironically, by the time I had made my way through grief to the point where I was able to explain "it" more clearly, I no longer needed anyone to "get it."

Being understood by others didn't matter once I thoroughly understood myself. It certainly would have helped, however, in those early years when the only people who seemed to understand many aspects of what I was going through were other widows.

One of the essays included in this book was written in my first year of widowhood. "Crossing Over" described the overwhelming sense of disconnection I felt from anyone who had not experienced great loss.

I came to realize that I didn't want to feel that sense of separation from others for the rest of my life. Grief Country is filled with those who have experienced death losses other than widowhood, and I wanted to feel connected to them, as well as those "on the outside," who have yet to experience a death loss. As upset as I get by people who equate non-death losses with death losses, I would still rather not wall myself off from them.

One of my reasons for writing this book was to try to build a bridge of understanding between those who have experienced widowhood and those who have not. We are separated on so many levels already—including but certainly not limited to politics, religion, ethnicity, and geographic identity—that it seems to me separating ourselves by our losses just widens the chasm between us.

There is still a veil between my friend and me, a thin layer of gauze that is almost imperceptible. We know it is there but our collective vision has improved so much through our strengthened friendship and mutual understanding that we can see through it if we try.

Perhaps I've stumbled into one of Grief Country's more rewarding areas, the State of Finding Meaning.

If the grief I have poured into sharing my story opens the eyes of someone who cares about a widow, it would give meaning to my loss.

We need to keep building bridges.

THE ROAD
(Written in Year One)

The open road is no friend of the bereaved
You wave goodbye, leaving Grief on the doorstep
like a forgotten suitcase
only to discover it has crept quietly into the back seat—
        a defiant stowaway

Too late to turn back
Memories litter the highway
Every milepost a marker of your life together
First glance
        first kiss
                first declaration of love

Your heart breaks in time
to the beat of the song on the radio
as Grief climbs, unnoticed, into the passenger seat

Look, there he is!
whispers Grief, edging ever closer
Those eyes that twinkled only for you!

You can almost reach out and touch his face
A crystal-clear reflection in the rearview mirror
Gone in one sun-blinding moment

As dusk falls it dawns on you
There are no exit ramps in sight
Will this wearying journey never end?

Grief nestles its head on your shoulder
while offering to take the wheel
But whatever you do
you must not pull over

THE ROAD (Continued)

Roll down the window
Let the cold night air revive you

Because if you hand over the keys
If you stop the car now
Make no mistake
You may never find your way
    back home again

FAR PAVILIONS

It had been a positive, uplifting four days. I had been invited to return to the town where I had once lived to talk about a book I had written about my experience with helping a community of refugees resettle in America.

I had also met with a community leader to discuss another possible book and spent time with my "second family"—once refugees, now U.S citizens. My heart had soared each time the children I had helped raise called me "Mama Stephanie." It had been too long since I had heard that honorific.

Old American friends had greeted me warmly. I had made a few new friends. Even the weather had been spectacular.

As I set out to make the nine-hour drive back home, I was feeling good—the best, in fact, that I had felt in a long time. I turned on the radio and settled on a station featuring "easy listening" that would maintain my calm, peaceful mood.

As the miles rolled by, I replayed the events of the past few days in my mind. I was proud of myself. My goal of becoming a writer was actually coming to fruition. I was establishing a new identity, an identity that had been supported by my husband when he was alive—but one that I was now faced with carving out on my own.

I peered through the windshield at the sky, the place where I always imagined Ron to be, hiding behind a stray cloud, watching over me. Of course he was proud of me, wherever he was.

The melodic strains of an Amy Grant song filled the car. I recognized it right away as her hit song, "I Will Remember You."

My calm, peaceful mood evaporated in an instant.

I began to cry.

Clutching the steering wheel, I tried to fight back my tears, but it was no use. There were few vehicles on this stretch of highway at this early hour, mostly semi-trucks whose drivers may or may not have noticed a middle-aged woman periodically wiping her eyes with a tissue while trying to continue driving.

Overcome with emotion, I cried out to my husband in the clouds. "I don't want this! I don't want any of this! I don't want to write stupid books! I don't want a new life! I just want you back! I want my life with you again!"

I was now crying in earnest. I had no business being on the road. Having traveled this highway dozens of times over the years, I knew I was close to a rest area.

Within a few minutes I was safely off the road, parked as far away as possible from the two or three other cars present. For the next ten or fifteen minutes I found myself sobbing uncontrollably, my head pressed against the tops of my hands, which were still clutching the steering wheel.

I had no idea why I had fallen apart so rapidly and unexpectedly. A psychologist might have been able to make something out of the emotions of returning to a place where my husband and I had lived, or feelings of conflict about trying to create a new identity.

Of course, Amy Grant's heartbreaking ballad hadn't helped.

Eventually the tears stopped and I leaned back against the headrest, telling myself to just breathe. I reached up, tilted the rearview mirror to the left, and was horrified by what I saw—mascara-smeared face, swollen, puffy eyes, red nose.

Sitting in my car in that Eastern Oregon rest stop, surrounded by brown, barren hills, I set about making repairs, using bottled water and tissues to avoid having to leave the car and encounter any strangers. As I reapplied all my makeup, I began to calm down. I could easily have foregone that exercise—after all, I was driving straight home—but the familiar routine brought me back to the normal world, the "new normal" world where I had to somehow find a way to go on without my beloved husband.

When I finished repainting my face, my personal suit of armor, I glanced a final time in the mirror and this time my eyes reflected not anguish but resoluteness. It was time to get back on the road.

As I slowly reentered the highway, I recognized the obvious metaphor. This is how it was going to be, traveling around Grief Country. There would be times I would simply break down and be forced to pull off the road, and I would never, even years after my husband's death, be able to accurately predict when that would happen. I needed to accept this and tell myself that it was okay.

But I also needed to get back on the road and continue on to my next destination. I could not let grief take control of the steering wheel.

The next time I returned to the town, my journey was not marred by any similar incidents. I breezed past the rest area on my way home, tossing it a quick glance while willing my mind not to go there, not to wander down the path of past stumbles off the road.

There is a state in Grief Country I have heard about, a place where the sun never sets on the hope for a brighter future.

There are no rivers of tears, only healing waters that envelop a widow in peace and acceptance.

It is a place where widows no longer lurk in the shadows of what used to be or what might have been. They step boldly into the sunshine, arms outstretched.

After five years I feel as if I'm getting closer to the State of Grace.

Some might argue that God has never withheld His blessings or favor from the bereaved, but to me, more than anything, widowhood and its aftermath felt like a spectacular fall from grace.

I was being punished over and over again for a sin I hadn't committed.

The hours I spent in the small church conference room with a handful of women of faith gradually helped to dispel that feeling. There were no "lightbulb" moments, no specific magic words that I carried with me when I departed, just a conviction that for an hour and a half, I had been in the presence of God. He did exist, and He did love me.

Eventually I carried that conviction out the door of the church conference room and into my life twenty-four hours a day.

The alchemy of my healing from grief has been a combination of the elements of faith, determination, hard work, support, self-sufficiency, and purpose.

Faith

One of the definitions of faith is having trust or confidence in someone or something. Over time I began to have faith that I would overcome the challenges that widowhood and its aftermath had presented. I began to have faith in myself.

Faith can also be a belief in God. Who can explain why they believe what they believe? Words are inadequate and, in any case, they do not constitute "evidence" in the traditional sense. I would only say that I began to see the hand of the Creator once more in my life. Although my restored faith did not translate into easy answers to the questions surrounding life and death, it gave me confidence that my story was not destined to end with my husband's death.

Determination

Determination is a gift I was given at birth. Determination helped me to survive an abusive childhood and other challenges. Usually I am the type of person who doggedly "soldiers on," bent on overcoming obstacles when they arise; however, I misplaced the gift of determination for a while when I lost my way after becoming a widow. Finding it again was key to continuing the fight for my life.

Work

When I use the word "work," I am referring to the concentrated effort of dealing with my psychological, emotional, and social needs as a widow given my specific circumstances.

Based on my family history, I knew that my highest priority needed to be my own mental health. I work hard to keep negativity out of my life. I work hard to redirect my thoughts away from debilitating sadness. I work hard to strengthen my resilience. I work hard to cultivate new, positive relationships, achieve goals, and help others. Do I have days when I cannot do any of these things? Yes, and I allow myself those days—sparingly. Then it's back to work.

Support

Reaching out for support was difficult for me in the early days of widowhood, primarily due to practical reasons. A perfect storm of circumstances—a recent move to a city where I had one friend, a lack of family support, and an ongoing role as a caregiver for my mother—left me adrift in a sea of isolation. Eventually I was able to supplement the support of my only local friend with grief and social groups, new friendships, and increased contact with my old out-of-state friends. My husband and I had relied primarily on each other for support, so the task of building a support network was time-consuming, not to mention daunting. After five years, however, I believe I've found a balance between support and self-sufficiency.

Self-sufficiency

Faith and self-sufficiency might strike some as mutually exclusive, but I see them as a winning combination. For me, being self-sufficient doesn't mean I don't rely on God. One definition of self-sufficiency is "being intellectually and emotionally independent." This means not relying on other human beings to direct my thoughts or control my emotions. Intellectual independence wasn't really an issue for me, but I had to work hard to become emotionally independent. It took several years for me to learn how to avoid letting the actions of others determine or influence my emotions.

Self-sufficiency did not preclude my need for support; however, I was careful to ensure that I did not rely too heavily on any one pillar of support. I had learned that lesson early in my widowhood journey. Supportive individuals can suddenly be consumed by the demands of their own lives, support group members can come and go, online groups can be unpredictable in nature and membership, and nonprofit organizations can unexpectedly close their doors.

Self-sufficiency means I know I will be just fine if any one pillar collapses. It can be replaced.

Purpose

Having a sense of purpose has been crucial to my healing—and a powerful balm for the pain. I was fortunate in that I had discovered my passions before my husband died. Many widows decide to become writers, but I was a fledgling writer who happened to become a widow. Finishing the book I had begun writing about my other passion—the Bantu refugees who had become my friends—gave me a sense of purpose, as did raising awareness about brain cancer and Alzheimer's disease through volunteerism.

In addition to the above factors, I credit following Stroebe and Shut's Dual Process Model of

Bereavement, as mentioned earlier in this book, with helping me along my journey. Balancing "loss-oriented activities" and "restoration-oriented activities" appealed to my proclivity for structure. "Taking time off from grief" enabled me to enjoy—without resentment—the company of those who were uncomfortable talking about my husband.

Loss-oriented activities—a fancy way to describe the tears that still come unbidden at times, and the overwhelming pressure I still feel in my chest when the missing and the yearning and the aching break out of their resting places and surge forth, demanding my attention. The loss-oriented activities have lessened, of course, but they have not disappeared from my life. I still miss him so.

The *restoration-oriented activities* of rebuilding my life without my husband have, on the other hand, actually increased over time. Widowhood is work, plain and simple, and it can often become harder as one ages. Dealing with financial pressures, addressing health issues, and other practical matters are especially challenging for older women who are alone.

Every widow has a unique combination of elements that fuel her progress through Grief Country. The elements that have helped me may not resonate with another widow. I honor every widow's unique path.

***

My road to widowhood was a fast-moving, terrifying route through aggressive brain cancer. The journey that followed has at times seemed inexorably slow, but it is growing easier as I near the State of Grace.

It is the most beautiful region of Grief Country. Like "The Far Pavilions," the three snow-capped peaks that beckoned the protagonist of the epic novel made famous by author M.M. Kaye,[1] the spectacular mountains that are looming in the distance are summoning me.

I picture these mountains as far pavilions of Optimism, Wisdom, and Perspective.

Optimism has at times been a struggle for a realist-at-birth such as myself. Can I find it again as a widow? I hope so.

Just when I think I have a modicum of Wisdom, humility finds a way to kick me in the backside. I continue to seek it, nonetheless.

Perspective is an elusive creature. It races in and out of my life with the speed of a cheetah. Perhaps it will take a few more years to acquire perspective about my widowhood journey.

Someday, when I reach these far pavilions of Optimism, Wisdom, and Perspective, I will stand atop the highest peak and wave the flag of widowhood I have now carried for five years. Then I will plant it firmly in the ground as a symbol that I have conquered Grief Country.

I may have to live in this land forever, but it is going to be on my terms. I plan to dwell in the most beautiful regions, the places where those who have grieved have found joy and peace, as well as a depth of compassion and understanding that enables them to be a light to others.

I think I just heard my husband whisper, *Atta girl!*

AFTERWORD

A year and a half after my husband Ron's death, I found a letter. A letter I had never seen before, one he had obviously begun to write sometime before his death. It contained a number of spelling errors, reflective of the effects of his illness. Brain cancer had robbed him of his short-term memory, and as I read the unsigned letter, I could visualize him setting it aside to finish at a later date. Or perhaps the letter was complete and he merely forgot to sign it. Or perhaps he purposely placed it in the stack of papers I was now sorting through with the intention that I would find it later.

I would never know, and it really didn't matter.

What did matter was his ongoing intention even during his illness to comfort and encourage me to go on with my life when he was gone.

I carry one sentence with me always, embedded in my mind and emblazoned onto my heart.

"Hopefully you will be able to feel my support in all you do."

I have felt his support every step of the way while writing this book.

And as I go forward, hopefully exploring aspects of life other than grief and loss, and opening myself up to whatever else this "Earth Walk" has to offer me, I know he will still be supporting me every step of the way.

NOTES

Anticipatory Grief

1. Erich Lindemann, "Symptomology and Management of Acute Grief," *American Journal of Psychiatry* 101 (1944): 141-148.

2. Therese A. Rando, "Living and Learning the Reality of a Loved One's Dying: Traumatic Stress and Cognitive Processing in Anticipatory Grief." In *Living With Grief When Illness is Prolonged*, edited by Kenneth J. Doka with Joyce Davidson. (Washington, DC: Hospice Foundation of America, 1997), 37.

3. Ibid.

4. University of Indianapolis, "Alzheimer's Care: Grief is Heaviest Burden for Caregivers." ScienceDaily. www.sciencedaily.com/releases/2008/03/08030620016.htm

Normal Grief

1. Stephen R. Schucter and Sidney Zisook, "The Course of Normal Grief." In *Handbook of Bereavement: Theory, Research and Intervention*, edited by Margaret S. Stroebe, Wolfgang Stroebe, Robert O. Hansson. (Cambridge: Cambridge University Press, 1997), 23.

2. J. William Worden, *Grief Counseling and Grief Therapy* (New York: Springer Publishing Company, 1991), 29.

3. Camille B. Wortman and Roxanne Cohen Silver, "The Myths of Coping with Loss," *Journal of Consulting and Clinical Psychology* 57:3 (1989): 351.

4. Margaret Stroebe and Henk Schut, "The Dual Process Model of Coping With Bereavement; Rationale and Description," *Death Studies*, 23:3 (1999): 216.

5. Stephen R. Schucter and Sidney Zisook, "The Course of Normal Grief." In *Handbook of Bereavement: Theory, Research and Intervention*, edited by Margaret S. Stroebe, Wolfgang Stroebe, Robert O. Hansson. (Cambridge: University Press, 1997), 24.

One Hundred Years of Grief

1. Sigmund Freud, "Mourning and Melancholia," Collected Papers (1917): 152-170. www.columbia.edu/itc/hs/medical/clerkships/psych/misc/articles/freud.pdf

2. Erich Lindemann, "Symptomology and Management of Acute Grief," *American Journal of Psychiatry* 101 (1944): 141-148.

3. Colin Murray Parkes, *Bereavement: Studies in Grief in Adult Life* (London: Tavistock, 1972), 29-105.

4. John Bowlby, *Loss: Sadness and Depression* (Attachment and Loss, Vol. 3). (New York: Basic Books, 1980), 85.

5. Elisabeth Kübler-Ross. *On Death and Dying* (New York: Simon and Schuster, 1969).

6. J. William Worden, *Grief Counseling and Grief Therapy* (New York: Springer, 1982), 11-16.

7. Therese A. Rando, *Treatment of Complicated Mourning* (Champaign: Research Press, 1993), 30-60.

8. Ibid., 43-60.

9. Thomas Attig, *How We Grieve: Relearning the World*. (New York: Oxford University Press, 1996), 44-46.

10. Dennis Klass, Phyllis R. Silverman, and Steven L. Nickman, *Continuing Bonds: New Understandings of Grief* (New York: Taylor & Francis, 1996).

11. Robert Neimeyer, *Lessons of Loss: A Guide to Coping*. (Boston: McGraw-Hill, 1998).

12. Margaret Stroebe and Henk Schut, "The Dual Process Model of Coping With Bereavement; Rationale and Description," *Death Studies*, 23:3 (1999): 215.

13. Robert Neimeyer, *Meaning, Reconstruction and the Experience of Loss*. (Washington, DC: American Psychological Association, 2001).

14. George A. Bonanno, "Loss, Trauma, and Human Resilience," *American Psychologist*, 59:1 (2004): 20-28.

15. Elisabeth Kübler-Ross and David Kessler. *On Grief and Grieving: Finding the Meaning of Grief Through*

the Five Stages of Loss (New York: Scribner, 2005), 11-17.

When Grief is Not Normal

1. American Psychiatric Association, *Diagnostic and Statistical Manual of Mental Disorders*, Fifth Edition. (Arlington, VA: American Psychiatric Association, 2013), 161.

2. Holly G. Prigerson and Paul K. Maciejewski, "Grief Intensity Scale," Weill Cornell Medicine Center for Research on End-of-Life Care. New York. https://endoflife.weill.cornell.edu/research/grief-intensity-scale

3. Kenneth J. Doka, ed. *Disenfranchised Grief: Recognizing Hidden Sorrow* (Lexington: Lexington Books, 1989).

Anger

1. George A. Bonanno, *The Other Side of Sadness: What the New Science of Bereavement Tells Us About Life After Loss* (New York: Basic Books, 2009), 36.

2. Mary S. Cerney and James R. Buskirk, "Anger: The Hidden Part of Grief," *Bulletin of the Menninger Clinic*, Spring: 55(2):228-37 (1991).

3. Elisabeth Kübler-Ross and David Kessler, *On Grief and Grieving: Finding the Meaning of Grief Through the Five Stages of Loss* (New York, NY: Scribner, 2005), 11-17.

The 6.5 Percent

1. U.S. Census Bureau, "Marital History for People 15 Years Old and Over by Age and Sex: 2009."

Resilience and Rebuilding

1. Kenneth J. Doka, *Grief is a Journey*. (New York: Atria Books, 2016), 59.

2. Ibid.

3. American Psychological Association, "The Road to Resilience." http://www.apa.org/helpcenter/road-resilience.aspx.

4. George A. Bonanno, "Loss, Trauma, and Human Resilience," *American Psychologist*, 59:1 (2004), 20-28.

A Show of Hands

1. Margaret S. Stroebe and Wolfgang Stroebe, "The Mortality of Bereavement: A Review." In *Handbook of Bereavement: Theory, Research and Intervention*, edited by Margaret S. Stroebe, Wolfgang Stroebe, Robert O. Hansson. (Cambridge: Cambridge University Press, 1997), 187-188.

2. National Alliance on Mental Illness. "Depression in Older Persons Fact Sheet." www/ncoa.org/wp-content/uploads/Depression_Older_Persons_Fact Sheet_2009.pdf

3. Richard Schulz, Randy Hebert and Kathrin Boerner. "Bereavement After Caregiving." *Geriatrics* 63:1 (2008), 20-22.

Research Has Shown...

1. Robert O. Hansson, Bruce N. Carpenter, and Sharon K. Fairchild. "Measurement Issues in Bereavement." In *Handbook of Bereavement: Theory, Research and Intervention*, edited by Margaret S. Stroebe, Wolfgang Stroebe, and Robert O. Hansson. (Cambridge: Cambridge University Press, 1997), 62.

2. Holmes, Thomas and Richard Rahe. "The Social Readjustment Rating Scale." *Journal of Psychosomatic Research* 11 (1967): 213-218.

Far Pavilions

1. Kaye, M.M. *The Far Pavilions*. (New York: St. Martin's Press, 1978).

Made in the USA
Monee, IL
07 July 2026